D0398559

The High Altitude Cookbook

The High Altitude Cookbook

by

Beverly Anderson Nemiro   *&*

Donna Miller Hamilton

RANDOM HOUSE, New York

FIRST PRINTING

Copyright © 1969 by Beverly Anderson Nemiro and
Donna Miller Hamilton

All rights reserved under International and
Pan-American Copyright Conventions.
Published in the United States by Random House, Inc.,
New York, and simultaneously in Canada
by Random House of Canada Limited, Toronto.

Library of Congress Catalog Card Number: 67-12738

Manufactured in the United States of America
by The Book Press,
Brattleboro, Vermont

Book design by Mary M. Ahern

To our mothers
Anna Mae Anderson & Verna Low Miller
for the tangible & intangible contributions of love,
loyalty & support

Acknowledgments

Grateful acknowledgment and appreciation are due to Miss Jackie Anderson, Cooperative Extension Service, Colorado State University, Denver, Colorado; Mr. Charles Bragaw, Technical Information Department, National Bureau of Standards, United States Department of Commerce, Boulder, Colorado; Mr. Frank Brzoticky, State Meteorologist, State of Colorado Weights and Measures Laboratory, Denver, Colorado; Department of Food Science and Nutrition, Colorado State University, Fort Collins, Colorado; Howard L. Enos, Extension Poultryman, Cooperative Extension Service, Colorado State University, Fort Collins, Colorado; Food Technologist and Manager of Quality Control, Kuner-Empson Company, Brighton, Colorado; Mr. Harold Gardner, Weights and Measures Inspector, City and County of Denver, Denver, Colorado; Mr. George K. Minor, Bakery Consultant, The Colorado Milling and Elevator Company Control Laboratory, Denver, Colorado; Mr. Jack D. Putnam, Chief Preparator, Denver Museum of Natural History, Denver, Colorado; Swift and Company, Food Information Service, Chicago, Illinois; Dr. Wilson K. Talley, Vice Chairman, Department of Applied Science, University of California, Davis, California; Mrs. Dora Anne Von Vihl, Mrs. Pauline Cleaver and Mrs. Francis Lyman, Home Economics Staff, The Emily Griffith Opportunity School, Adult Vocational and Technical Education Division of the Denver Public Schools, Denver, Colorado.

Contents

The High Altitude Cookbook

Introduction

Don't despair if you live 2,500 feet or more above sea level and have encountered failures when using recipes from your favorite cookbook or recipe file. You haven't lost your touch. It's the *altitude*.

Recipes designed for use at sea level frequently give less-than-perfect results at higher altitudes. Yet you can readily convert your favorite recipes or correct disheartening mistakes by learning to cope with and compensate for the altitude.

Briefly, here are some key factors which affect cooking and baking at altitudes of 2,500 feet and higher, and a few general rules that follow from them. As elevation increases, atmospheric pressure decreases, humidity decreases, and the rate of evaporation of liquids speeds up. Just as the pressure of water is greater at the bottom of the sea than at the surface, so the pressure of air is greatest at sea level, or below, decreasing as the altitude increases. This causes water to boil at 202°F. at 5,000 feet, for example, instead of at 212°F. as at sea level. This means that the temperature of the water surrounding the egg you are boiling will never be as hot as it is at sea level. The same is true for the sauce cooking in the top of a double boiler; the soup or stew you are simmering; or the liquids within the meat, fish, fowl or vegetable you are baking: none will cook at the same temperature as at a lower altitude. What should be done?

Since boiling liquids are less hot, it follows that it will take longer for foods to cook to the desired doneness. But while you are cooking foods longer, the atmosphere is busily drying out the moisture in the food at a greater rate because of the low humidity in high places. Therefore, it is essential that more water or other liquids be used in stove-top cookery and that a watchful eye be kept on the kettle to keep its contents from cooking dry or scorching.

No matter how high you turn up the stove burner, the food you are cooking cannot get any hotter than the boiling point of water where you are, so you lengthen the cooking time. Because boiling is involved when canning foods and blanching produce before freezing, processing time is increased. In baking and oven cookery, however, the temperature *can* be raised. But proper balance of oven temperature and time is important, lest foods become burned. In cake and bread baking, balance of ingredients is very important. For example, leavening is decreased because the lighter air at high altitudes allows doughs and batters to rise more and faster. Additional liquid is called for because flour tends to dry out in low-humidity regions lying far above sea level. The use of moisture-retaining agents such as buttermilk and sour cream is helpful in high-altitude recipes.

Not all high-altitude cooking problems can be solved by a longer cooking time or use of a higher baking temperature. Candies, frostings and jellies take less cooking time because rapid evaporation causes sugar solutions to become concentrated sooner than at lower elevations, and overcooking causes them to become too done or hard. Another exception is deep-fat frying which is most successful at high elevations if the temperature of the cooking oil or fat is lowered.

For each kind of cooking there are material helps that you shouldn't try to live without. Heavy saucepans with tight-fitting lids and heavy-duty aluminum foil help preserve moisture. A meat thermometer will tell the exact internal temperature of meat and a candy thermometer helps judge the doneness of syrups after subtractions are made for the differences in atmospheric pressure. Some persons consider a pressure cooker a necessary tool at high altitudes.

This sketch will help you to understand the problems of high-altitude cooking and points toward general solutions. However, your best help will come from the recipes and charts in this book. The recipes have been time-tested and family-tested. Temperatures have been adjusted and ingredients balanced for success at high altitudes. You will find them reliable helps.

Happy eating in this wide—and high—world.

B. A. N.
D. M. H.

Guide to
Successful Cooking
at High Altitudes

Appetizers: See individual subject matter. Covering with aluminum foil or placing in covered chafing dish insures warmth without evaporation.

Baking Powder: Double-acting baking powder (sodium aluminum sulfate) was used in testing the recipes in this collection. It is recommended for high-altitude use as it reacts slowly in the cold mixture and releases most of its leavening power in baking. Substitute 1½ teaspoons of other types (tartrate or calcium phosphate) of baking powder for 1 teaspoon double-acting baking powder. Fresh baking powder works best.

Boiling: The higher the altitude the lower the boiling point of water, necessitating the use of *furiously* boiling water at all times and increasing the length of cooking time for vegetables, soups, stews, and the like. At very high altitudes a pressure cooker may be necessary. See Pressure Cooker.

Braising: An especially good method for cooking meat, poultry, game and vegetables above sea level. Lightly brown in small amount of fat, then cook in heavy pan or baking dish with tight-fitting cover in liquid (water, stock, vegetable juices).

Breads, Quick: Slightly decrease baking powder in standard recipes. More liquid may be necessary, or use sour cream or buttermilk. Breads made with fruits are particularly successful, as they do not dry out rapidly.

Breads, Yeast: Compensate for drying out of flour at high altitudes by using less flour or by adding more liquid. Watch rising dough carefully, punching it down when it is just doubled in bulk, as yeast rises more rapidly above 2,500 feet. A little more baking time may be needed. Brush crust lightly with softened butter or oil, if desired.

Broiling: Intense heat quickly seals in juices and prevents dryness. Care must be taken to baste larger pieces of meat and poultry frequently. Lengthen broiling time. See Marinades.

Cakes: Use only recipes that have been ingredient-balanced and adjusted for high altitudes. The special directions for high altitude on packaged cake mixes should be followed. One school of thought is to make high-altitude adjustments according to package directions, then add 2 tablespoons cooking oil to small packages and 4 tablespoons to larger packages. In baking, cake flour is preferable. Avoid using "wonder" type flours. Use of butter, high-grade margarines, emulsified or hydrogenated shortenings as well as sour cream and buttermilk make up for dryness in atmosphere. Do not overbeat eggs or batter. An extra egg often helps. Beat egg whites until stiff, but not dry. Generously grease pans, or line them with waxed paper and grease the paper as cakes are more inclined to stick above sea level. Frost as soon as possible to preserve moisture. See High-Altitude Adjustments for Sea-Level Cake Recipes, page 16, and High-Altitude Leavening Adjustments for Sea-Level Cake Recipes, page 17.

Cakes, Cup: Cake batters make excellent cup cakes. To prevent sticking, use paper baking cups or grease cup cake pans generously. Bake about 20 minutes. See Cakes.

Cakes, Sponge: Do not overbeat eggs or egg yolks. Use a little less leavening if any other than air is called for. Addition of an extra egg often strengthens and stabilizes batter. See Cakes and Angel Food Cake Deluxe, page 229.

Candies: Decrease cooking time to prevent too-concentrated syrup. Avoid scorching. The quickened concentration of liquid and sugar where the air is thinner and drier hastens scorching of sugar syrups. Dissolve sugar carefully over low heat before beginning of cooking. An excellent method for determining the amount of cooking required by candies at high altitude is the cold-water method of testing: Drop ½ teaspoon boiling syrup into a cup of very cold water. Candy is at soft-ball stage when syrup can be picked up and formed into soft ball that flattens; at firm-ball stage when syrup can be formed into a solid, but not hard, ball that holds shape unless pressed; at hard-ball stage (the last stage) when a ball can still be formed or shaped before the soft-crack stage is reached; at that point, syrup separates into hard, but not brittle, threads. See High-Altitude Temperature Guide for Candy Making, page 18.

Canning: Canning processes are affected at high elevations because of the lower boiling temperature of water. Therefore, an increase in processing time is necessary. The general rule is to add 1 minute to the processing time for each 1,000 feet in elevation, if the processing time is more than 20 minutes. See High-Altitude Time Corrections for Canning, page 15.

Cereals: Add a few minutes of cooking time and a little extra liquid to offset evaporation. Avoid using a double boiler, if possible; a heavy saucepan with a tight-fitting cover is preferable. Stir frequently to avoid hazard of sticking.

Chafing-Dish Cookery: Ideal for warming or keeping cooked foods warm; not heartily recommended for actual cooking.

Charcoal Cookery: As a form of broiling and rotisserie cookery, this method is highly satisfactory. See Broiling.

Coffee: A longer brewing time is needed to compensate for the lower boiling point of water. A high-enough temperature must be reached and held until sufficient infusion has taken place. Set automatic coffee maker for medium-strong-to-strong coffee, then adjust it to individual preference if the result is too strong. When brewing on stove top, use higher heat and brew longer. Coffee cools more rapidly the higher one gets, so make use of coffee warmers and heavy mugs or insulated cups. Brew instant coffee in a pot rather than individual cups, as there is not enough heat to bring about dissolving and flavor-releasing action.

Coffee Cakes: See Breads (Quick and Yeast) and Cakes.

Cookies: Sometimes a slight reduction in leavening and in sugar is needed for best quality. Butter, high-quality emulsified and hydrogenated shortenings, brown sugar, cream and sour cream are helpful moisturizers. Do not over-measure dry ingredients, or overbake cookies. If dough seems too dry, add a small amount of water or milk. Do not use too much flour when rolling out cookie dough. Store in airtight containers.

Cream of Tartar: Be sure your supply is fresh for best results.

Deep-Fat Frying: Because of the lower boiling point of the water (moisture) in the foods to be fried, the cooking temperature of oil must be lowered to 350°–360° F., and cooking time increased a little. A too-high temperature will produce a crusty exterior and underdone interior.

Desserts: Generally increase time and/or temperature in making cooked desserts, either on stove top or in the oven. A little more liquid in batters or pastries may be needed to prevent dryness. A heavy saucepan over direct heat is preferable to a double boiler for making custards and puddings, particularly to obtain maximum gelatinization of cornstarch.

Double Boiler: Because of the lowered boiling point of water at elevations above 2,500 feet, a double boiler cannot be used without expending an extra amount of time. A heavy-bottomed saucepan over low or medium heat is a more satisfactory method if a careful watch is kept against scorching and sticking.

Doughnuts: Use a lower frying temperature—350°–360° F. See Deep-Fat Frying.

Dumplings: Use ample broth for cooking. Slightly increase amount of liquid in recipe and increase cooking time.

Eggs: All egg cookery takes longer at high altitudes, but do not increase heat in cooking omelets and frying eggs. A 3-minute egg will take 4 minutes at 5,000 feet. In frying eggs, use a heavy skillet. To poach an egg takes 4 to 6 minutes, or longer. All recipes in this book call for large eggs, unless otherwise noted. Beat egg whites only until stiff but not dry.

Fish: Use of ample butter, wine, sauces, court bouillon, fumet, as well as frying in batter, help to maintain moisture. Aluminum foil seals in natural juices—in fact, some believe cooking fish in foil is the best way at high altitudes. When sautéeing, pan-frying and broiling, be careful not to overcook. Leaving head and tail on when baking whole fish helps to retain natural juices. Poaching is excellent.

Flour: Unless otherwise specified, all-purpose flour should be used. Avoid granulated ("wonder type") flours.

Foil Cookery: Aluminum foil is excellent for making tent-type coverings for large roasts or poultry; for wrapping of meats, fish, poultry or vegetables to seal in moisturing juices and liquids, and is useful for covering leftovers or as a pan covering if a tight-fitting lid is unavailable.

Freezing: See Preparing and Processing Vegetables for Freezing, page 30. Water blanching (scalding) or steam blanching is necessary to inactivate harmful bacteria at higher elevations.

Fricasseeing: Because of moist heat, recommended for cooking less tender poultry and cuts of meat and game. Increase liquid and cooking time.

Fritters: Judge when done by appearance. Use cooking temperature lowered to 350°–360° F. See Deep-Fat Frying.

Frosting: Watch cooked frostings closely above 2,500 feet. The thinner air allows them to reach the done stage more quickly. See Candies.

Game: Cook calf elk like veal, adult elk like beef. Choice cuts of venison and antelope can be roasted or broiled like beef. Unpalatable dryness is prevented by using less tender cuts in stews, fricassees or pot roasts; or prepare with marinades, gravies or sauces. See Meats.

Game Birds: See Poultry. The natural dryness in some birds and, frequently, the questionable age of wild birds, ducks and geese that makes them less tender are coupled with the hazards of high altitude. A practical approach is to cook game birds with sauces, gravies and wines. See Fricasseeing.

Gravies: Allow extra cooking time over medium-low heat to avoid a raw taste in thickened gravies. Cook the roux before adding liquid. Direct heat and a heavy saucepan or skillet are preferable to a double boiler for gravy making.

Jellies and Jams: Jelling point comes sooner at high altitudes. A candy thermometer is recommended. Lower the finish temperature by 1.90° F. for each 1,000 feet in elevation (220° F. would be adjusted to 210.5° F. at 5,000 feet, for example).

Legumes, Dried: Need additional cooking time and the addition of liquid frequently. A heavy pan with tight-fitting cover is helpful to avoid sticking and scorching. At elevations over 8,000 feet a pressure cooker is almost a necessity. See Soups.

Marinades: Very important, as marinating game, meats and poultry adds moisture. Highly recommended for meats, poultry and game. Marinade soaks into and is absorbed, thereby keeping moisture and juices intact. Use to baste while roasting or broiling, or as liquid when braising.

Meats: Careful time and temperature adjustments necessary. Add moisturizers (wine, sour cream, consommé, broth, sauces) and increase cooking time. Use heavy saucepans, skillets, and Dutch ovens with tight-fitting covers. Baste frequently with pan juices. Use meat thermometer. Avoid cooking dry. See timetables for roasting meats, pages 19–25; Braising, Broiling, Foil Cookery, Fricasseeing, Marinades, Pots, Pans, and Baking Dishes, Pressure Cooker, Sautéeing, and Stewing.

Muffins: See Breads.

Pancakes: Packaged or homemade high-altitude pancakes need more liquid, and some experienced cooks recommend an extra egg. Especially good when made with sour cream or buttermilk. Do not overmix.

Pastas: Package directions are inadequate for cooking above 2,500 feet. Macaroni, noodles, spaghetti and other pastas need added cooking time and extra liquid to be done and tender. Always use *furiously* boiling water, and add salt after it reaches a boil. The addition of 2 tablespoons cooking oil to water is recommended.

Pies: Evaporation of liquid and drying out of flour in pie dough may be remedied by a little additional liquid. Bake fruit and berry pies a bit longer. Increase baking temperature 10 to 15 degrees. Use as small an amount of flour as possible when rolling out dough.

Poaching: Excellent to defeat dryness of rarefied atmosphere, especially for fish.

Popovers: Made by sea-level recipes, these expand too rapidly. Eggs should be increased and shortening omitted or reduced.

Pots, Pans, and Baking Dishes: Heavy-duty cooking pots and pans with tight-fitting covers help prevent scorching and evaporation of moisture. Cast iron, cast iron with enamel, heavy-duty aluminum or iron with non-stick coatings, pyroceram, heavy-duty glassware and heavy-duty stainless steel with copper-bottom pots, pans and baking dishes are most satisfactory. See Double Boiler.

Poultry: Baste frequently, or use moist-heat methods of cooking, with increased cooking time. Sauces, gravies, marinades, wines, canned cream soups and sour cream add moisture. See High-Altitude Timetable for Roasting Poultry, page 24.

Pressure Cooker: Increase pressure 1 pound for each 2,000 feet above sea level, and increase cooking time 5 per cent for every 1,000 feet above the first 2,000 (15 per cent at 5,000 feet, for example). Increased pressure within the cooker raises the temperature at which the water boils and causes food to cook more rapidly. Some authorities believe a good pressure cooker is a necessity for some types of high-altitude cookery, such as canning (to kill botulinus organisms) and for dried legumes.

Rotisserie Cookery: See Broiling.

Rice: Increase cooking time and amount of liquid called for in package directions. To judge doneness, pinch a grain or two between fingertips. Rice should feel soft, not mushy.

Sauces: Recommended heartily to preserve moisture of foods. See Gravies and Marinades.

Sautéeing: Pan-frying in a very little fat is a necessary step in many recipes and is especially effective for sealing in precious juices. Caution must be used not to scorch or dry out product in sautéeing. Use heavy skillet.

Soups: Because the boiling point of liquids cannot be raised by turning the burner to higher heat, soups must be cooked longer or be processed in a pressure cooker if they are to become completely flavor-melded and thoroughly cooked. The longer cooking necessary on the top of the range means more chance of evaporation. Remedies for this are to keep a watchful eye on soup liquids; to add more water or liquid as needed; to maintain a constant simmer or slow boil; to use a pot or kettle with a tight-fitting cover.

Steamed Puddings: A pressure cooker processes steamed puddings more quickly than a pot, and eliminates need for frequent additions of water to produce steam.

Sterilizing: Jelly glasses, canning jars, baby bottles, and other items to be sterilized should be processed in water kept at a furious boil. Several extra minutes' sterilizing time is required to kill harmful bacteria.

Stewing: A heavy saucepan or a Dutch oven with tight-fitting cover is essential to prevent rapid evaporation. Add more liquid from time to time, as needed.

Stuffings: Use flavorful liquids such as wine, broth, canned soups, bouillon or consommé, as well as butter, cream and eggs, to keep stuffings as well as poultry moist.

Tea: To compensate for the lower boiling point of liquids, tea must be made with *furiously* boiling water in a preheated pot, and allowed to steep longer than at sea level. See Coffee.

Vegetables: See Soups and High-Altitude Timetable for Cooking Vegetables, page 26.

Waffles: Do not overbeat egg whites. See Pancakes.

Yeast: Rises more rapidly above 2,500 feet. Use cake yeast only when fresh. Active dry and cake yeast are interchangeable. Watch rising dough carefully, letting rise only until just doubled in bulk.

Charts

HIGH-ALTITUDE TIME CORRECTIONS FOR CANNING IN BOILING-WATER BATH

Standard instructions for canning foods in a boiling-water bath must be adjusted for high altitudes, as shown in this table.

Caution: Before tasting or serving any home-canned meat, fish or vegetable, bring food to a full, rolling boil for at least:

    10 minutes at sea level
    15 minutes at 5,000 feet
    20 minutes at 8,000 feet or above
    20 minutes for spinach and corn at all altitudes.

Elevation	If time called for is less than 20 minutes, add:	If time called for is greater than 20 minutes, add:
Sea level	0 minute	0 minute
1,000 feet	1 minute	2 minutes
2,000 feet	2 minutes	4 minutes
3,000 feet	3 minutes	6 minutes
4,000 feet	4 minutes	8 minutes
5,000 feet	5 minutes	10 minutes
6,000 feet	6 minutes	12 minutes
7,000 feet	7 minutes	14 minutes
8,000 feet	8 minutes	16 minutes
9,000 feet	9 minutes	18 minutes
10,000 feet	10 minutes	20 minutes

Vegetables other than tomatoes and pickled beets may take 15 hours or more at sea level to destroy or inactivate the spores or bacteria at boiling temperature. If cooked in a pressure cooker, they are destroyed in less than 1 hour. Therefore, non-acid vegetables (other than tomatoes) and meats should always be processed in the pressure cooker. See Pressure Cooker, page 13, for high-altitude time corrections.

HIGH-ALTITUDE ADJUSTMENTS FOR SEA-LEVEL CAKE RECIPES

Decrease each measurement the lesser amount at the lowest altitude and the larger amount at highest altitude within the given range.

Adjustment	At 2,000 to 3,500 feet	At 3,500 to 5,000 feet	At 5,000 to 6,500 feet	At 6,500 to 8,000 feet
For each teaspoon of baking powder, baking soda, or cream of tartar, decrease by:	¼ to ⅓ teaspoon	⅓ to ½ teaspoon	½ to ⅔ teaspoon	⅔ to ¾ teaspoon
For each cup of sugar, decrease by:	1 to 1½ tablespoons	1½ to 2½ tablespoons	2½ to 3 tablespoons	3 to 3½ tablespoons
For each cup of liquid, increase by:	0 to 2 tablespoons	2 to 3 tablespoons	3 to 4 tablespoons	4 to 6 tablespoons
Increase cake flour by:	—	1 tablespoon	2 tablespoons	3 tablespoons
Increase baking temperature by:	—	15° to 25°F.	15° to 25°F.	25°F.

Begin adjustment for your altitude by reducing baking powder, baking soda, or cream of tartar. Liquid and flour adjustments may not be necessary after adjusting the leavening; this can be determined by experience. Very rich cake batters may be better if shortening is decreased 1 to 2 tablespoons.

HIGH-ALTITUDE LEAVENING (BAKING POWDER AND BAKING SODA) ADJUSTMENTS FOR SEA-LEVEL CAKE

Recipes Used Above 2,000 Feet

Use larger amount of leavening at lower altitude.
Use smaller amount of leavening at higher altitude.

Sea-Level Measurement	At Altitudes 2,000 to 3,500 Reduce To:	At Altitudes 3,500 to 5,000 Reduce To:	At Altitudes 5,000 to 6,500 Reduce To:	At Altitudes 6,500 to 8,000 Reduce To:
1 teaspoon	¾ to ⅔	⅔ to ½	½ to ⅓	⅓ to ¼
1½ teaspoons	1¼ to 1	1 to ¾	¾ to ⅔	⅔ to ½
2 teaspoons	1¾ to 1½	1½ to 1¼	1¼ to 1	1 to ¾
2½ teaspoons	2 to 1¾	1¾ to 1½	1½ to 1¼	1¼ to 1
3 teaspoons	2¼ to 2	2 to 1½	1½ to 1¼	1¼ to 1
3½ teaspoons	3 to 2½	2½ to 2	2 to 1½	1½ to 1
4 teaspoons	3 to 2½	2½ to 2	2 to 1½	1½ to 1

HIGH-ALTITUDE TEMPERATURE GUIDE FOR CANDY MAKING

Type of Candy	Cold-Water Test	Candy Thermometer Reading for:		
		2,000 feet	5,000 feet	7,500 feet
Creams Fudges Fondants	Soft-ball stage	230°F. to 236°F.	224°F. to 230°F.	219°F. to 225°F.
Caramels	Firm-ball stage	238°F. to 244°F.	232°F. to 238.5°F.	227°F. to 233°F.
Divinities Taffies Caramel popcorn	Hard-ball stage	246°F. to 264°F.	240°F. to 258°F.	235°F. to 253°F.
Butterscotch English toffees	Soft-crack stage	266°F. to 286°F.	260°F. to 286°F.	255°F. to 275°F.
Brittles	Hard-crack stage	296°F. to 306°F.	290°F. to 300°F.	285°F. to 295°F.

HIGH-ALTITUDE TIMETABLE FOR ROASTING BEEF

Refrigerate beef up to time of roasting. Preheat oven. Place roast on rack in shallow pan. Do not cover, baste or add water. Place meat thermometer in center of thickest part of meat, not touching bone or fat. (Because roasts of the same weight usually vary in shape and in fat and bone content, a meat thermometer is the most accurate means of judging when a roast is done.) Roasting times per pound given in this chart are also sound guidelines for determining when meat has reached desired doneness. Also see Meats, page 12.

Allow roasts to stand 15 to 20 minutes out of oven before carving.

Serving allowances: For boneless meat, allow ¼ pound per serving. For meat with average amount of bone, allow ½ pound per serving. For bony meat, allow 1 pound per serving.

Beef Cut	Weight (pounds)	Oven Temperature (preheated)	Roasting Time in Minutes per Pound	Meat Thermometer Reading
Standing Rib; Sirloin	5½ to 8	325°F.	20 to 25	140°F.—Rare
			25 to 30	160°F.—Medium
			30 to 35	170°F.—Well done
Rolled Rib	4	325°F.	30 to 35	140°F.—Rare
			35 to 40	160°F.—Medium
			40 to 45	170°F.—Well done
Tenderloin (Fillet)	4	450°F.	10 to 12	130°F.—Rare
			13 to 15	150°F.—Medium
			16 to 18	160°F.—Well done

HIGH-ALTITUDE TIMETABLE FOR ROASTING HAM AND FRESH PORK

Refrigerate meat up to time of roasting. Preheat oven. Place in shallow pan or on meat rack. Do not cover, baste or add water. Place meat thermometer in thickest part of meat, not touching bone or fat. (Because roasts of the same weight usually vary in shape and in fat and bone content, a meat thermometer is the most accurate means of judging when a roast is done.) Roasting times per pound given below also provide sound guidelines for determining when meat has reached a desired doneness. Also see Meats, page 12.

Allow either ham or pork roasts to stand 15 to 20 minutes out of oven before carving.

Serving allowances: For boneless meat, allow ¼ pound per serving. For meat with average amount of bone, allow ½ pound per serving. For bony meat, allow ¾ to 1 pound per serving.

Ham

	Weight (pounds)	Oven Temperature (preheated)	Approximate Roasting Time (hours)	Meat Thermometer Reading	Additional
Uncooked whole	10 to 15	325°F.	4 to 5¾	170°F.	Add 10 minutes per pound if boned and rolled
Uncooked half	4 to 8	325°F.	2¼ to 3½	170°F.	Add 10 minutes per pound if boned and rolled
Precooked whole	10 to 12	325°F.	2½ to 3	140°F.	
	12 to 15	325°F.	3 to 3½	140°F.	
	15 to 18	325°F.	3½ to 4	140°F.	

	Weight (lbs.)	Oven Temperature	Hours	Internal Temperature	
Precooked half	5 to 8 8 to 10	325°F. 325°F.	1½ to 2⅓ 2⅓ to 3	140°F. 140°F.	
Uncooked whole picnic	5 to 8 8 to 10	325°F. 325°F.	3 to 4 4 to 5	170°F. 170°F.	
Canned *or* precooked rolled	3 to 5 5 to 8	325°F. 325°F.	1 to 1⅔ 1⅔ to 2¼	140°F. 140°F.	
Fresh Pork					
Loin	2 to 3 5 to 7	325°F. 325°F.	1⅔ to 2½ 3½ to 4½	185°F. to 190°F. 185°F. to 190°F.	Add 10 minutes per pound if loin is boned and rolled
Shoulder (Picnic or Boston butt)	4 to 6	325°F.	3½ to 4½	185°F. to 190°F.	Add 10 minutes per pound if shoulder is boned and rolled
Crown (unstuffed)	4 to 6	325°F.	3½ to 4½	185°F. to 190°F.	

HIGH-ALTITUDE TIMETABLE FOR ROASTING LAMB AND MUTTON

Refrigerate meat up to time of roasting. Preheat oven. Place meat in shallow pan on meat rack. Do not cover, baste or add water. Place meat thermometer in thickest part of meat, not touching bone or fat. Because roasts of the same weight usually vary in shape and in fat and bone content, a meat thermometer is the most accurate means of judging when a roast is done. Roasting time per pound also provides sound guidelines for determining when meat has reached a desired doneness. Also see Meats, page 12.

Allow roast to stand 15 to 20 minutes out of oven before carving.

Serving allowances: For boneless meat, allow 1/4 pound per serving. For meat with bone, allow 1/2 pound per serving.

Cut	Weight (pounds)	Oven Temperature (preheated)	Approximate Roasting Time (hours)	Meat Thermometer Reading
Leg	6	325°F.	2 to 2½	150°F. to 155°F.—Rare
	6	325°F.	2¼ to 2¾	160°F.—Medium
	6	325°F.	2½ to 3	165°F. to 175°F.—Medium-well
	6	325°F.	3½	175°F. to 180°F.—Well done
Rack	4 to 5	325°F.	2⅓ to 3¾	175°F.—Medium-well
Crown (unstuffed)	3 to 5	325°F.	1¾ to 3	170°F. to 172°F.—Medium
Shoulder	3 to 5	325°F.	2 to 3	175°F.—Medium-well
Cushion	4 to 5	325°F.	2⅓ to 2⅔	180°F.—Well done
Boned and Rolled	3 to 5	350°F.	2¼ to 3¾	175°F.—Medium-well

HIGH-ALTITUDE TIMETABLE FOR ROASTING VEAL

Refrigerate up to time of roasting. Preheat oven. Cover veal roast with thin slices of salt pork, suet or fat bacon if it lacks a fatty coating. Place in shallow pan on meat rack. Do not cover, baste or add water. Place meat thermometer in thickest part of meat, not touching bone or fat. Because roasts of the same weight usually vary in shape and in fat bone content, a meat thermometer is the most accurate means of judging when a roast is done. Roasting time per pound also provides sound guidelines for determining when meat has reached a desired doneness. Also see Meats, page 12.

Allow roasts to stand 15 to 20 minutes out of oven before carving.

Serving allowances: For boneless meat, allow ¼ pound per serving. For meat with average amount of bone, allow ½ pound per serving. For bony meat, allow 1 pound per serving.

Cut	Weight (pounds)	Oven Temperature (preheated)	Approximate Roasting Time (hours)	Meat Thermometer Reading
Leg	5 to 7	325°F.	3 to 4	170°F.
Loin	5	325°F.	3 to 3½	170°F.
Shoulder	3 to 5	325°F.	2 to 3¼	170°F.
Boned and rolled leg, loin or shoulder	4	325°F.	3⅓	170°F.

HIGH-ALTITUDE TIMETABLE FOR ROASTING POULTRY

Refrigerate poultry up to time of roasting. Preheat oven. Stuff just before roasting, if stuffing is used. For unstuffed poultry, a general rule is to reduce roasting time slightly, or about 2 to 5 minutes per pound depending on size of bird. Also see Poultry, page 13. Allow small birds to stand 10 minutes and large birds to stand 15 to 20 minutes out of oven before carving.

Poultry	Ready-to-Cook Weight (before stuffing)	Oven Temperature (preheated)	Roasting Time* (stuffed)
Chicken	2 to 3½ pounds	325°F.	1½ to 2½ hours
	4 to 5 pounds	325°F.	2½ to 3½ hours
Duckling	3½ to 5 pounds	325°F.	2 to 3 hours
Goose	4 to 8 pounds	325°F.	3¼ to 4¼ hours
Turkey (in uncovered pan)	6 to 8 pounds	325°F.	3½ to 4 hours
	8 to 12 pounds	325°F.	4 to 5 hours

	12 to 16 pounds	325°F.	5 to 5½ hours
	16 to 20 pounds	325°F.	5½ to 6½ hours
	20 to 24 pounds	325°F.	6½ to 7½ hours
Turkey (wrapped in foil)	6 to 8 pounds	450°F.	2 to 2½ hours
	8 to 12 pounds	450°F.	2½ to 3 hours
	12 to 16 pounds	450°F.	3 to 3½ hours
	16 to 20 pounds	450°F.	3½ to 4 hours
	20 to 24 pounds	450°F.	4 to 5 hours
Squab	¾ to 1 pound	350°F.	1 hour
Capon	5 to 8 pounds	325°F.	3 to 4½ hours
Rock Cornish hen	¾ to 1 pound	325°F.	1 to 1¼ hours

* Times vary according to individual birds and ovens.

HIGH-ALTITUDE TIMETABLES FOR COOKING VEGETABLES

For 1 pound fresh (trimmed) or 1 package (9 to 10 ounces) frozen vegetables

Boiled Fresh Vegetables: Bring water to boil. Add ½ teaspoon salt and prepared vegetables to water. Cover pan closely. Reduce heat to medium-low. Begin timing.

Boiled Frozen Vegetables: Bring water to boil. Add ½ teaspoon salt to water. Add vegetables. Allow water to come to second boil. Cover pan. Reduce heat to medium-low. Begin timing. (If following package directions for frozen vegetables, add a few minutes' cooking time and a little additional liquid.)

Baked Frozen Vegetables: Add 2 tablespoons butter or margarine, ½ teaspoon salt and vegetables to water. Cover baking dish. Stir once or twice during baking. To bake in foil, place frozen vegetables in center of sheet of heavy aluminum foil, add 2 tablespoons butter or margarine and ½ teaspoon salt. Seal package by folding foil tightly. Baking times given are for 350°F. If baking at 325°F, increase time 12 minutes. If baking at 375°F, decrease time 7 minutes.

Vegetable	FRESH		FROZEN		
	Boiling Time (tightly covered) (*minutes*)	Amount of Water	Boiling Time (*minutes*)	Amount of Water	Baking Time at 350°F. (tightly covered)
Artichoke (globe)	30 to 45	to depth of 1 inch			
Artichoke hearts	20	1 cup	5 to 10	1 cup	
Asparagus					
cuts	12 to 15	to depth of 1 inch	10	¼ cup	1 hour
spears	14 to 20	to depth of 1 inch	11	¼ cup	1 hour

Beans					
Green, French style					
or cut	25 to 30	1 cup	14	½ cup	1 hour
Green, whole	30 to 40	1 cup	15	½ cup	1 hour
Lima, large	20 to 30	1 cup	15	1 cup	1 hour
Lima, baby	20 to 30	1 cup	15	1 cup	1 hour
Wax	25 to 30	1 cup	12	¼ cup	1 hour
Italian	25 to 30	1 cup	7	½ cup	1 hour
Beets (small whole)					
young	30 to 50	to cover			
old	60 to 90	to cover			
Broccoli					
cuts	20	to depth of 1 inch	7	¼ cup	45 minutes
spears	25	to depth of 1 inch	8	¼ cup	1 hour
Brussels sprouts	15	1 cup	10	¾ cup	1 hour
Cabbage					
shredded	5 to 10	to depth of ¾ inch			
quartered	12 to 20	to depth of ¾ inch			
Carrots					
diced	20	1 cup	10	¼ cup	45 minutes
sliced	25	1 cup	14	¼ cup	45 minutes
baby whole	30	1 cup	16	¼ cup	1 hour

Vegetable	FRESH		FROZEN		
	Boiling Time (tightly covered) (minutes)	Amount of Water	Boiling Time (minutes)	Amount of Water	Baking Time at 350°F. (tightly covered)
Cauliflower					
flowerets	12 to 15	¾ cup	10	½ cup	45 minutes
whole	25	1 cup		½ cup	1¼ hours
Celery, sliced	15 to 25	to depth of 1 inch			
Corn					
kernel	5 to 6	½ cup	8	¼ cup	45 minutes
on the cob I	5 to 10	to cover	(thawed) 8	to cover	45 minutes
on the cob II	6 to 12	to depth of 1 inch			
Greens					
Spinach	12	to depth of ½ inch	8	½ to 1 cup	1 hour
Beet, mustard, chard, etc.	12 to 18	to depth of ½ inch	16	½ to 1 cup	1 hour
Mixed vegetables	Cook and mix		14	½ cup	1 hour
Okra	15 to 30	1 cup	10 to 12	¼ cup	1 hour
Onions, small whole or large quartered	25 to 35	to cover			

Vegetable					
Parsnips, halved or quartered	25 to 35	1 cup			
Peas					
green	15 to 20	½ cup	12	¼ cup	45 minutes
black-eyed	60	1 cup	60	2 cups	1½ hours
Peas and carrots	Cook separately and mix.		12	¼ cup	55 minutes
Potatoes					
cut up	25 to 30	to cover			
whole	45	to cover			
sweet (whole, in jackets)	45	to cover			
Rutabagas	See Turnips				
Spinach	See Greens				
Squash					
summer	25	½ cup	15	¼ cup	1 hour
winter: acorn halves or Hubbard pieces	45	1 cup	20 to 30	none (use double boiler)	1 hour
Succotash	Cook separately and mix.		15	½ cup	1 hour
Tomatoes, quartered	10 to 15	¼ cup			
Turnips, sliced or cubed	20 to 30	1 cup			

PREPARING AND PROCESSING VEGETABLES FOR FREEZING AT HIGH ALTITUDES

This table is for elevations up to 5,000 feet. At elevations of 5,000 or more feet, allow 1 minute longer processing time.

Vegetable	Preparation	Processing Time To:	
		Water Blanch (*scald*)	Steam Blanch
Asparagus	Wash. Cut off woody bases, remove scales, if sandy, and sort according to size of stalk.	Small stalks, 2 minutes Large stalks, 4 minutes	2½ minutes 4 minutes
Beans (green or snap)	Wash. Remove ends and strings. Sort according to size and cut lengthwise, slantwise or crosswise; or leave whole.	Cut beans, 2 minutes Whole beans, 3 minutes	2 minutes 3 minutes
Beans (lima)	Shell, wash and sort according to size.	Small beans, 2 minutes Large beans, 3 minutes	
Beets	Cut tops off short. Cook in salted water until tender. Cut off stems and roots, slip off skins, cool, and pack in containers whole, sliced or diced.		
Broccoli	If necessary to draw out insects, soak in salt water 20 to 30 minutes. Wash, trim off large leaves, split into 1-inch-thick pieces, and cut off the bases of longer stalks to fit container.	Small stalks, 3 minutes Large stalks, 5 minutes	3 minutes 5 minutes
Brussels sprouts	If necessary to draw out insects, soak in salt water 20 to 30 minutes. Wash carefully, remove loose outer leaves, and sort by size.	Small, 3 minutes Medium, 4 minutes Large, 5 minutes	
Carrots	Cut off tops, wash, scrape, and cut into 1¼-inch slices.	Slices, 3 minutes Small, whole, 5 minutes	3½ minutes 5½ minutes

Vegetable	Preparation		
Cauliflower	Wash, divide into flowerets, and sort according to size.	Small flowerets, 3 minutes Large flowerets, 4 minutes	4 minutes 5 minutes
Corn (on the cob)	Use only young corn. Husk and sort according to size.	Small ears, 6 minutes Medium ears, 8 minutes Large ears, 10 minutes	
Corn (kernel)	Husk. Sort by size. Process only 6 ears at a time. Cool, then cut off kernels, scraping cob with back of knife to extract milk.	Same as corn on cob	
Greens (beet, chard, collards, mustard, spinach)	Wash under running water to remove sand and grit. Discard bruised leaves, cut off tough stems. Process small amount at a time and pack lightly in containers.	2 minutes	
Mixed vegetables	Prepare and process separately. Combine after cooling.		
Mushrooms	Wash quickly. Cut off stems at base of cap. Treat for darkening (see Spiced Peaches, page 000), and sort according to size.	Small buttons or quarters, 3 minutes Medium, whole, 4 minutes	3½ minutes 5 minutes
Peas	Wash pods. Shell, and discard any shriveled or dry peas.	Small peas, 1 minute Large peas, 1½ minutes	1⅓ minutes 2 minutes
Peppers (green or red sweet)	Wash, remove seeds and halve, if desired.	2 minutes	
Squash (summer)	Freeze immediately after picking. Wash, cut in ½-inch slices.	Until tender (use salted water)	4 minutes
Squash (winter and pumpkin)	Cook until tender in salted water, or steam. Mash or press through sieve and cool.		

2

HIGH-ALTITUDE OVEN TEMPERATURE CHART
(Fahrenheit and Centigrade)

Oven	Degrees Fahrenheit	Degrees Centigrade
Slow	300°F. to 325°F.	149°C. to 163°C.
Moderate	340°F. to 375°F.	177°C. to 191°C.
Hot	400°F. to 425°F.	204°C. to 218°C.

BOILING POINT OF WATER FROM SEA LEVEL TO 14,000 FEET

Height above sea level	Boiling point of water (F.)
0	212.0
500	211.0
1000	210.0
1500	209.1
2000	208.2
2500	207.1
3000	206.2
3500	205.3
4000	204.4
4500	203.4
5000	202.6
5500	201.7
6000	200.7
6500	199.8
7000	198.7
7500	198.0
8000	196.9
10000	194.0
12500	189.8
14000	187.3

33

To determine the boiling point of water where you live:

Find the altitude at which you live on the bottom line. Using a ruler, draw a line from this point upward to meet the slanting line. Mark where your line meets the slanting line. Using the ruler, draw a straight line from the marked point to the Boiling Point of Water scale. Where the line joins the scale indicates the Centigrade and Fahrenheit temperatures of boiling water at your elevation (see example below).

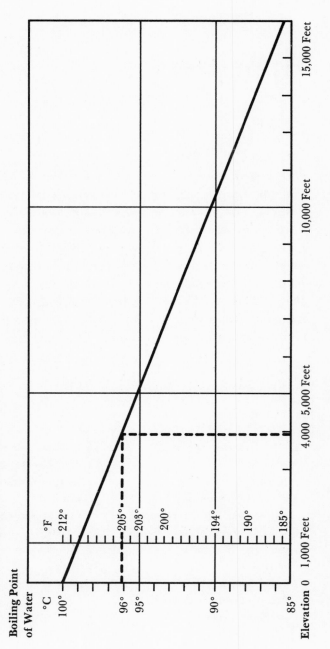

Boiling Point of Water

Appetizers

The experienced cook at altitudes above 2,500 feet realizes that the dry atmosphere has undesirable effects on many appetizers. The remedies are simple. Chafing dishes will help to keep foods warm but are inadequate for the total cooking process because of the lower boiling point of liquids. Keep prepared hors d'oeuvres under freshness-preserving wraps— plastic or aluminum foil—as the drying air is a quick thief of the vital moisture in meats, breads, spreads and the like. Use warming stands or dishes for hot tidbits and keep them covered, or the quick-cooling atmosphere will leave them cold.

Braunschweiger Pâté
About 2 cups

1 tablespoon unflavored gelatin
1 tablespoon water
1 can (10½ ounces) condensed beef consommé
6 stuffed green olives, sliced
1 package (8 ounces) cream cheese
1 roll (8 ounces) braunschweiger sausage *or* good liverwurst

⅛ teaspoon paprika
¼ teaspoon seasoned pepper
¼ teaspoon dried sweet basil, crumbled
1 tablespoon chopped parsley
2 tablespoons lemon juice
Lettuce
Parsley clusters

1. Soak gelatin in water for 5 minutes.
2. Heat consommé. Add gelatin. Cool. Pour ¼ cup consom-mé into a 2- or 3-cup mold, swishing it up sides. Stud with stuffed olive slices. Refrigerate until set.
3. Beat together cream cheese, braunschweiger, paprika, pepper, sweet basil, parsley and lemon juice. Blend with remaining consommé, mixing until smooth.
4. Pour over jelled consommé in mold. Refrigerate until set.
5. Unmold onto bed of lettuce on a chilled serving dish. Garnish with parsley.

Planked Beef Tenderloin and Canadian Bacon

20 or more servings

1 beef tenderloin (about 4 pounds)	1 piece Canadian-type bacon (about 3 pounds)
¼ cup firmly packed brown sugar	3 tablespoons water
¼ cup pineapple juice	20 Parker House or potato rolls, cut in half and buttered

1. Preheat oven to 350°F. Have 2 shallow baking pans ready.
2. Trim beef of any fat. Place in baking pan.
3. Mix brown sugar with pineapple juice. Cover Canadian bacon with mixture. Place in second separate pan with 3 tablespoons water.
4. Place meats in preheated oven. Remove beef after 15 minutes. Allow Canadian bacon to heat through (about 20 minutes).

5. Meanwhile, preheat broiler. Place beef under preheated broiler, turning to brown quickly on all sides, about 5 minutes altogether.
6. Place broiled beef and Canadian bacon side by side on wooden serving plank or heated platter. Slice thinly. Serve 1 slice beef and 1 slice bacon on each buttered roll.

Broiled Cocktail Kebabs

In making kebabs, use your imagination to invent tasty combinations of meats, fish, shellfish, fruits, or vegetables. Choose items that take the same length of time to cook. Prepare kebabs ahead, refrigerate until needed, then broil under a preheated broiler. Use metal or wood skewers that will not let foods slip during broiling, baking, or barbecuing.

Some suggested combinations:

Chunks of lobster alternated with chunks of beef tenderloin (page 35)

Scallops, pineapple chunks and stuffed green olives.

Chicken livers and cocktail sausages.

Frankfurters cut into diagonal chunks, blanched small onions and cherry tomatoes.

Stuffed olives and chunks of white-fleshed fish.

Oysters wrapped in bacon and cherry tomatoes.

Squares of steak marinated in Teriyaki Sauce, page 163, and cherry tomatoes.

Chunks of cooked chicken and eggplant, both marinated in French dressing or Teriyaki Sauce, page 163.

Stuffed olives, canned peach chunks and cooked shrimp.

Chunks of cooked ham, pineapple chunks and green pepper.

Cocktail onions (pickled) and chunks of frankfurters.
Chunks of kidney and cocktail sausages.
Chunks of lobster and unpeeled apple.

Cocktail Burgers

2 dozen

1 pound lean ground beef
chuck or round steak
¼ pound pork sausage
⅓ cup fine dry bread crumbs
⅓ cup dry sherry
¼ cup cream
2 tablespoons finely chopped
green onion, if desired

1 tablespoon finely chopped
parsley
1 teaspoon seasoned salt
½ teaspoon seasoned pepper
Shortening or cooking oil
Cocktail-size hamburger buns,
or baking-powder biscuits
Piquant Sauce, page 162, or
sauce of your choice

1. In mixing bowl combine meats, bread crumbs, sherry, cream, onion, parsley, salt and pepper. Toss together until blended. Shape into thin 1-inch patties.
2. In skillet, sauté patties in shortening or cooking oil until browned on both sides. Drain.
3. Serve in cocktail-size bun, sandwich style, or atop halves of small biscuits, secured with toothpicks. Add dab of Piquant Sauce or other sauce, if desired.

Cocktail Meat Balls: Form meat mixture into 1-inch balls. Sauté as directed and serve on a heated platter or in a chafing dish, with toothpicks for spearing. Serve with Piquant Sauce, page 162, or Barbecue Sauce, page 154.

Camembert-Roquefort Mousse

2 cups, or about 6 servings

1 tablespoon unflavored
gelatin
¼ cup water
3 wedges (1⅓ ounces each)
Camembert cheese,
softened
2 wedges (1¼ ounces each)
Roquefort cheese, softened

1 teaspoon Worcestershire
sauce
1 egg, separated (beat white
until stiff but not dry)
½ cup whipping cream,
whipped
Parsley or watercress

1. Lightly oil a 2-cup mold.
2. In custard cup, soften gelatin in water. Place cup in simmering water until gelatin dissolves.
3. With fork, blend cheeses, Worcestershire sauce and egg yolk until quite smooth. Add gelatin and mix.
4. Fold beaten egg white and whipped cream into cheese mixture. Pour into mold. Refrigerate until firm.
5. Unmold onto serving plate. Garnish with parsley or watercress and serve with soda or crisp rye crackers.

Cheese Puffs

20 canapés

2 egg whites, beaten until
stiff but not dry
1 cup grated American
cheese

1½ teaspoons Worcestershire
sauce
½ teaspoon paprika
½ teaspoon dry mustard
20 1-inch rounds of bread

1. Preheat broiler.
2. Into beaten egg whites fold cheese, Worcestershire sauce, paprika and mustard. Mix lightly until smooth.

3. Toast bread rounds on one side. Spread untoasted side with cheese mixture.
4. Broil until golden and puffed. Serve very hot.

Chili con Queso

(Chili with Cheese)   8 to 10 servings

1 cup chopped onions
3 tablespoons butter
1½ cups chopped ripe
  tomatoes *or* drained and
  chopped canned tomatoes
1 can (4 ounces) green
  chili peppers, chopped

1 teaspoon salt
½ teaspoon pepper
1 pound grated American
  cheese
Tomato juice, if necessary
Toasted tortillas *or* corn chips

1. In heavy saucepan, sauté onions in butter until limp.
2. Add tomatoes, chili peppers, salt and pepper. Simmer over low heat for 5 minutes.
3. Add cheese. Stir until melted.
4. Thin with tomato juice, if too thick.
5. Serve hot as a dip for oven-heated tortillas or corn chips.

Stuffed Mushrooms

2 dozen

24 large mushrooms, washed
  and dried
½ cup melted butter
Juice of 1 lemon
 2 tablespoons minced parsley
 2 tablespoons minced onion

¼ cup grated Swiss cheese
½ teaspoon salt
Dash freshly ground pepper
¾ cup fine bread crumbs
¼ cup sherry

1. Preheat oven to 350°F. Lightly butter a baking sheet.
2. Cut stems from mushrooms. Dip caps in melted butter, using ¼ cup. Sprinkle with lemon juice.
3. Make stuffing: Chop mushroom stems very fine. In skillet, sauté chopped mushroom stems, parsley and onion in remaining ¼ cup melted butter until limp.
4. Combine grated cheese, salt, pepper, ½ cup bread crumbs and sherry. Add sautéed vegetables. Toss lightly.
5. Shake lemon juice from mushroom caps. Fill each cap with stuffing. Sprinkle lightly with remaining ¼ cup bread crumbs. Dot with additional butter. Place on prepared baking sheet.
6. Bake at 350°F. for 15 to 20 minutes. Serve piping hot.

Shrimps Gourmet

Sauce for 1 pound cooked shrimp

⅔ cup good mayonnaise (not salad dressing)
1 tablespoon plus 1 teaspoon cream
Dash Worcestershire sauce
2 tablespoons catsup
4 drops liquid hot pepper sauce
Dash freshly ground pepper
3 tablespoons dry sherry
1 teaspoon fresh lemon juice
1 tablespoon plus 1 teaspoon cognac
1 teaspoon finely chopped parsley

1. In blender or small bowl of electric mixer, blend ingredients in order listed until smooth.
2. Use as dip for boiled shrimp, or pour sauce over shrimp and serve as an appetizer.

Beverages & Soups

Tea and Coffee

Tea brewing and coffee making give constant reminders of the effects caused by water boiling at a lower point at higher elevations. At 5,000 feet, the temperature of boiling water is 9.5°F. lower than at sea level. To compensate, tea must be made with furiously boiling water in a preheated *pot, and allowed to steep longer than at sea level. When using an automatic coffee maker, set the regulator between medium-strong and strong, then adjust it to individual preference if the coffee is too strong. Also see Coffee, page 9.*

Hot Spiced Chocolate
6 servings

6 tablespoons cocoa	⅛ teaspoon salt
¼ teaspoon ground cinnamon	½ cup sugar
	¼ cup water
⅛ teaspoon ground allspice	5 cups milk *or* 4 cups milk
⅛ teaspoon ground cloves	and 1 cup coffee cream

4 1

1. In 2-quart saucepan combine cocoa, cinnamon, allspice, cloves, salt, sugar and water.
2. Over low heat, boil gently for 4 minutes, stirring frequently.
3. Add milk or milk and cream. Heat, but do not boil, until tiny bubbles form around edge.

Mexican Chocolate: Omit allspice and cloves. In Step 1, add 3 teaspoons instant coffee powder. Add 1 teaspoon vanilla extract just before serving.

Hot Mulled Burgundy Wine

10 to 15 servings

3 cups strong hot tea
1 cup sugar
2 lemons, sliced
18 whole cloves
3 sticks (2-inch) cinnamon

2 bottles (⅘ quart each)
　Burgundy wine
Ground nutmeg
Orange slices
Lemon slices
Whole cloves

1. In 2-quart saucepan combine hot tea, sugar, lemon slices, cloves and cinnamon. Cook over medium-low heat for 15 minutes. Remove from heat.
2. Strain spiced tea into 4-quart enamel or stainless-steel saucepan. Add Burgundy wine.
3. Heat, but do not boil, over low heat.
4. Serve in punch bowl. Sprinkle top with nutmeg and decorate with orange and lemon slices studded with cloves.

Hot Cranberry Punch: Substitute 1 quart cranberry-juice cocktail and 1 quart pineapple juice for Burgundy wine.

Sangría

(Spanish Wine Punch)   About 2 quarts

⅓ cup sugar
 1 quart red wine
   (Burgundy or claret)
 1 orange, sliced
 1 lemon, sliced

1 lime, sliced
1 peach, sliced
1 bottle (28 ounces)
  sparkling soda water,
  chilled

1. In large pitcher or other container, dissolve sugar in wine. Add fruit. Refrigerate at least 4 hours.
2. Before serving add sparkling soda water. Serve from ice-filled pitcher.

All-Season Fruit Punch

6 to 8 servings
Serve in individual glasses or in a punch bowl, hot or cold.

 2 cans (6 ounces each)
   frozen grapefruit *or*
   grape juice
4½ cups water
 1 cup sugar
 ¼ cup fresh lemon *or*
   lime juice
 1 teaspoon ground allspice
 ¼ teaspoon ground nutmeg
 ¼ teaspoon ground cloves

 8 canned, fresh *or* frozen
   pineapple sticks, if punch
   is to be served in glasses,
   or 8 canned or fresh
   pineapple slices, if to be
   served in punch bowl
24 whole cloves
 1 quart ginger ale
   (for cold punch only)

For hot punch: In 2-quart saucepan mix grapefruit or grape juice with water, sugar, lemon or lime juice, allspice, nutmeg and cloves. Bring just to boiling point, then simmer over low heat for 3 minutes. Pour into 6 to 8 preheated individual mugs, cups or glasses. Garnish each serving with a pineapple stick studded with 3 cloves.

For cold punch: Chill hot juice mixture. When cool, add ginger ale. Pour over ice in glasses, or into a punch bowl containing a ring or block of ice. Garnish each glass with a pineapple stick studded with 3 cloves, or garnish the bowl with pineapple slices studded with 3 cloves each.

Rum Fruit Punch: Add 1 cup rum after simmering the juices.

Borscht

6 servings

Borscht, Borsch, or Borsht? Whichever way you spell the name of this Russian vegetable soup, it is uniquely and interestingly flavored. Serve it chilled or piping hot, depending on your mood and the temperature of the day.

1 pound beef brisket, cut into 6 pieces	1½ cups canned tomatoes, *or* 1 can (6 ounces) tomato paste
6 cups water *or* 4 cups Beef Stock (page 46) *or* diluted canned bouillon	1 bay leaf
	1 tablespoon salt
1½ cups chopped onion	2 tablespoons vinegar
1½ cups thinly sliced carrots	1 tablespoon sugar
2 cups washed and thinly sliced beets	2 cups finely shredded cabbage
	Dairy sour cream

1. In large kettle, place beef and water, stock or bouillon. Cover. Bring to boil, skim, then simmer over low heat for 2½ hours, or until beef is tender. Add onion, carrots, beets, tomatoes or tomato paste, bay leaf and salt. Simmer for 30 minutes. Skim off fat.
2. Add vinegar, sugar and cabbage. Cover. Simmer until cabbage is tender.
3. Serve hot in individual bowls topped with 1 tablespoon sour cream; or refrigerate and serve chilled, topped with sour cream.

Cold Cherry Soup with Wine

6 servings

An exotic beginning or a sweet ending for a summer dinner. Top each serving with a dollop of dairy sour cream or whipped cream if the meringue puffs are omitted.

2 cans (1 pound each) red tart cherries, drained	½ teaspoon grated orange rind
2 cups water	1⅛ cups sugar
1 stick cinnamon	1 cup claret *or* other dry red wine
2 whole cloves	1 tablespoon brandy
	4 eggs, separated

1. In medium-size saucepan with cover, simmer cherries with water, cinnamon, cloves, orange rind and 1 cup sugar for about 20 minutes, or until flavors are well blended. Remove cloves and cinnamon stick.
2. Add wine and brandy. Bring to simmering point; remove from heat.

3. Beat egg yolks well with 1 tablespoon sugar. Blend a little hot soup into egg yolks, then beat yolk mixture into rest of soup.
4. Beat egg whites with 1 tablespoon sugar until stiff but not dry. Drop egg whites by tablespoonsful onto hot soup.
5. Cover. Remove from heat and allow to stand 1 hour. Refrigerate overnight.
6. Served chilled with one of the meringue puffs atop each serving; or top, as suggested above, with sour or whipped cream.

Beef Stock

About 6 cups

Renowned chefs make frequent use of a stock pot into which they put bones, vegetable liquids, celery tops and good odds and ends of meat. When simmered for hours and strained, it provides a deep-flavored stock base for soups, sauces, stews and the like.

3 pounds combined brisket (or other stew beef) and shin bone *or*
3 pounds soup meat and bone
1 cup chopped onion
1 cup chopped carrot
1 cup chopped celery stalks and leaves

½ cup chopped turnips, if desired
½ cup chopped green pepper, if desired
1 tablespoon salt
⅛ teaspoon pepper *or* 3 peppercorns
1 bay leaf, if desired
Water
Beef extract, if desired

1. In large soup kettle with tight-fitting cover, or in pressure cooker, place meat and bones, onion, carrot, celery, turnips and green pepper, salt, pepper or peppercorns, bay leaf and water to cover. If desired, first brown meat and bones in a small amount of fat in kettle or pressure cooker, then add vegetables, seasonings and water.
2. Bring to a boil, skim, lower heat and simmer 3 hours over medium-low heat; or cook in 15 pounds pressure, 30 minutes at 5,000 feet, letting pressure drop of its own accord. (See Pressure Cooker, page 13, for additional information, altitude and time adjustments.)
3. Strain through fine sieve. Correct seasoning. Add beef extract for color, if desired. Chill. Skim off fat.
4. Stock keeps well, refrigerated, for several days; or it may be frozen for longer storage.

Shrimp, Crab or Oyster Gumbo

6 to 8 servings

2 tablespoons butter
2 tablespoons all-purpose flour
4 cups Beef Stock, page 46, *or* canned chicken broth
¼ cup chopped onion
1½ cups drained canned tomatoes
3 cups thinly sliced okra
1 clove garlic, minced

4 teaspoons Worcestershire sauce
1 to 2 cups cooked rice
½ green pepper, seeded and thinly sliced
1½ pounds shelled raw shrimp, crab *or* oysters, *or* ½ pound each shrimp, crab and oysters
Chopped parsley

1. In heavy 2-quart saucepan with cover, melt butter over low heat. Stir in flour. Cook 2 to 3 minutes.
2. Add stock or broth, blending well. Add onion, tomatoes, okra, garlic, Worcestershire sauce, rice, green pepper and seafood.
3. Cover. Simmer over low heat until vegetables and seafood are done and seasonings are blended.
4. Serve with garnish of chopped parsley.

Cream Soup Base

6 servings

This base requires vigorous stirring and longer cooking to reach smoothness at high altitudes. Chicken stock gives depth to its flavor.

1½ cups chicken stock or broth	1 teaspoon grated onion, if desired
1 cup half-and-half cream	Salt
2½ tablespoons butter	Pepper
1½ tablespoons all-purpose flour	Paprika, if desired

1. In heavy-bottomed 1-quart saucepan, combine chicken stock or broth and cream. Heat, but do not boil.
2. Make roux: In small skillet melt butter over low heat, but do not brown. Add flour. Stir over low heat until smooth and slightly cooked—2 to 3 minutes. Add hot liquid to roux little by little, blending until smooth. Cook, stirring constantly over medium-low heat until smoothly thickened and well cooked—8 to 10 minutes.
3. Season to taste with salt, pepper and paprika, if desired. More cream may be added, if desired.

Cream of Peanut Soup: Add ½ cup chunk-style peanut butter to hot Cream Soup Base.

Clam Bisque: In Step 2, add 1 tablespoon minced carrot with onion. Add 1 can (10½ ounces) minced clams and liquid to Cream Soup Base.

Cream of Chicken Soup: Cook ½ cup chopped celery, 1 tablespoon chopped parsley and ¼ teaspoon paprika with 1½ cups chicken broth until celery is tender. Add broth mixture and ½ to 1 cup cooked or canned shredded chicken to Cream Soup Base. Garnish with chopped chives, if desired.

Fresh Pea Soup

4 servings

2 cups fresh or frozen peas	3 cups chicken broth
1 small onion, sliced	2 tablespoons all-purpose
1 cup water	flour
½ teaspoon salt	½ cup whipping cream
⅛ teaspoon pepper	Fresh mint, finely chopped

1. In saucepan combine peas, onion, water, salt and pepper. Cook until peas are tender. Drain peas, reserving liquid. Press peas through sieve.
2. Blend ½ cup chicken broth with flour until smooth. Add remaining chicken broth and liquid from peas. Cook over low heat, stirring constantly, until thickened and well cooked. Add peas. Bring to boil. Add cream.
3. Serve hot; or chill and serve ice-cold, garnished with fresh mint.

Split Pea Soup

6 to 8 servings

The higher the altitude, the more difficult it is to get dried peas, beans and lentils cooked to that nice soft stage. It was sheer frustration to old prospectors to find their beans never would get "done" when their camps were above 10,000 feet. Many homemakers find the pressure cooker the most satisfying solution for faster, complete cooking of dried legumes. This method eliminates the hazard of the vegetables, cooking dry and the need for long vigilance over the soup pot.

The following ingredients and amounts are a starting point. The quantity of water required is large because of the coalition of dried legumes and dry air.

2 cups dried split peas	1 cup chopped celery
2 or 3 quarts water	1 bay leaf
1 ham bone and meat, *or*	1 clove garlic, minced,
turkey carcass, *or*	if desired
½ pound ham pieces, *or*	Few grains cayenne pepper,
1½ pounds ham hocks, *or*	if desired
¼ pound piece salt pork or	2 teaspoons salt
bacon, *or*	½ teaspoon pepper
2 to 4 frankfurters, sliced	2 tablespoons all-purpose
1 large onion, chopped	flour, if desired
1 large carrot, chopped	

1. Place split peas in colander or sieve. Wash thoroughly.
2. *Stovetop method:* Place peas in large soup kettle with tight-fitting cover. Soak overnight in water to cover well. Drain. Return to kettle. *Pressure-cooker method:* Wash peas and place in pressure cooker.
3. Add 2 to 3 quarts water, meat or meat and bones (except

frankfurters) , onion, carrot, celery, bay leaf, garlic and cayenne pepper. (Do not add salt now, as it toughens dried legumes, changes their flavor and slows the cooking.)

4. *Stovetop method:* Cook, covered, over medium-low heat for 3 hours or more, adding water when necessary and stirring occasionally. Peas should be tender and somewhat mushy. *Pressure-cooker method:* Cook at 15 pounds pressure, 35 minutes at 5,000 feet, letting pressure drop of its own accord. (See Pressure Cooker, page 13, for additional information, altitude and time adjustments.)

5. Add salt and pepper. Remove bay leaf.

6. According to personal preference, peas may be "bruised" (slightly mashed) and liquid cooked down to desired consistency for serving, or flour may be mixed with a little liquid and blended into soup and cooked a few moments to thicken.

7. If using frankfurters, add last and reheat soup.

New England Clam Chowder
6 servings

3 dozen shucked large
  clams and liquid *or*
2 cans (10½ ounces each)
  minced clams and liquid
¼ pound bacon or salt pork,
  diced
2 medium onions, sliced
3 cups thinly sliced
  potatoes

Water
1½ teaspoons salt
¼ teaspoon pepper
3 cups scalded milk *or*
  1 cup scalded whipping
  cream and 2 cups scalded
  milk

1. Swish fresh clams in their juice to loosen any sand. Lift out, drain (saving all juice) and chop. Strain juice through cheesecloth to eliminate sand.
2. In deep kettle, brown diced salt pork or bacon until crisp. Remove and reserve.
3. Add onions to drippings. Sauté until light brown. Add potatoes and water just to cover. Cook until almost tender. Add salt and pepper.
4. About 10 minutes before potatoes are done, add fresh or canned clams and liquid. When potatoes are tender add scalded milk or scalded cream and milk, and reheat just to boiling point.
5. Add cooked bacon or salt pork, if desired, and serve hot.

Cheese Soup

6 servings

⅓ cup butter	1½ cups milk, water, chicken
1 cup grated carrots	stock *or* broth
1 cup finely chopped celery	Dash Worcestershire sauce
2 tablespoons grated onion	Dash nutmeg
½ cup chopped watercress,	Cream Soup Base, page 48
if desired	½ pound American cheese,
	melted

1. In medium-size skillet melt butter over low heat. Add carrots, celery, onions and watercress, if desired. Cook until limp but not browned.
2. Add milk, water, chicken stock or broth, Worcestershire sauce and nutmeg.
3. Combine with hot Cream Soup Base. Beat in cheese.
4. Serve hot.

Gazpacho

8 servings

1 medium onion
1 thinly peeled cucumber, cut up
1 green pepper, stemmed and seeded
4 cups tomato juice
Juice of 2 limes
1½ tablespoons wine vinegar
1½ tablespoons Worcestershire sauce
1 drop liquid hot pepper sauce

1 small clove garlic, mashed or pressed
¾ teaspoon salt
⅛ teaspoon pepper, preferably freshly ground
2 hard-cooked eggs
¼ teaspoon dry mustard
2 tablespoons salad or olive oil
Sliced limes

1. Finely grind, using food chopper or blender, the onion, cucumber and green pepper. Add tomato juice, lime juice, vinegar, Worcestershire, and liquid hot pepper sauce, garlic, salt and pepper.
2. Mash hard-cooked eggs. Mix eggs, mustard and oil to paste. Add to soup.
3. Blend well in blender, or vigorously beat with rotary or electric beater.
4. Chill for at least 2 hours. Serve with an ice cube and a slice of fresh lime in each helping. Improves after one or more days in refrigerator.

Breads

Above sea level, yeast doughs must be carefully watched to avoid overproofing (rising too high). Allow to rise just until doubled in bulk, or as instructed in the recipes in this section.

White Bread

2 loaves

1 package active dry yeast
  or 1 fresh cake compressed yeast
1¼ cups lukewarm water
1 cup scalded milk
1 tablespoon melted shortening

1 tablespoon melted butter
2 tablespoons sugar
2 teaspoons salt
6 to 6½ cups sifted all-purpose flour
Melted butter *or* shortening *or* cooking oil

1. In bowl large enough to accommodate raised dough, sprinkle dry yeast or crumble compressed yeast into ¼ cup lukewarm water. Stir to dissolve.
2. Into scalded milk mix melted shortening, melted butter, sugar, salt and remaining 1 cup water. Stir until dissolved. Cool to lukewarm. Add to yeast mixture.
3. Add one third of sifted flour. With electric mixer set at

54

low speed, or with a spoon, beat batter until smooth and satiny. Add remaining flour gradually, changing from mixture or spoon to hands as the dough becomes stiffer.

4. Turn dough onto floured board. Knead until elastic (tight-feeling), smooth and no longer sticky enough to adhere to board; or continue to knead in mixing bowl until all flour and dough are cleaned from sides of bowl by kneading process.

5. Grease same bowl and replace dough in it. Brush exposed surface with melted butter, shortening or cooking oil. Cover with damp cloth, leaving edges outside bowl. Let rise in warm place (about 80°F.) until doubled in bulk.

6. Punch down dough. Work the edges to center, turn bottom side up and knead very lightly. Lightly grease top, re-cover with damp cloth and let rise again until almost doubled in bulk.

7. Preheat oven to 425°F. Grease two 9 x 5 x 3-inch loaf pans.

8. Punch down dough, knead lightly, and divide into two equal parts. Shape into loaves. Place in prepared pans. Brush tops with melted butter, shortening or cooking oil. Re-cover with damp cloth. Let rise until center of dough is well rounded above pan, or until just doubled in bulk.

9. Bake at 425°F. for 15 minutes, then *reduce* temperature to 350°F. and bake 30 to 35 minutes longer or until done. (Bread is done when it shrinks from pan sides and sounds hollow when thumped on sides.) Turn out immediately to cool on wire rack or across top of pans. Brush with melted butter, if desired.

Anise-Seed Bread: Follow directions for White Bread. Reduce water to 1/4 cup and use to dissolve yeast. Increase milk to 2 cups. Increase butter to 1/2 cup and sugar to

6 tablespoons. In Step 2, add 1 beaten egg and 2 tablespoons anise seed.

Peanut-Butter Bread: Follow directions for White Bread. In Step 2, substitute ½ cup peanut butter for butter and shortening.

Swedish Light Rye Bread: Follow directions for White Bread. In Step 1, reduce water to 1 cup and use to dissolve yeast. Blend in 1 cup unsifted rye flour. Let this sponge rise and fall, or let rise overnight. In Step 2, substitute 1 cup boiling water for milk and 1 cup firmly packed dark-brown sugar for granulated sugar. Add 2 tablespoons caraway seed or 1 teaspoon anise seed. In Step 3, reduce all-purpose flour to 4½ cups. Add 1 cup rye flour. Bake in oven preheated to 350° F. for about 45 minutes.

Oatmeal Bread

2 loaves
Potato water and oatmeal are effective moisturizers.

1 cup cooked, thick oatmeal
2 cups hot potato water
¼ cup mashed potatoes
¼ cup dark molasses
2 tablespoons melted lard or shortening
1 package active dry yeast *or* 1 fresh cake compressed yeast
¼ cup lukewarm water
5 cups sifted all-purpose flour
½ cup less 2 teaspoons sugar
1½ teaspoons salt
Melted butter or shortening

1. In bowl large enough to accommodate raised dough, mix together oatmeal, potato water, mashed potatoes, molasses and melted shortening. Let stand 1 hour.

2. Sprinkle dry yeast or crumble fresh yeast into lukewarm water. Stir to dissolve. Add to oatmeal mixture.

3. Add one third of sifted flour and all of sugar and salt to oatmeal mixture. With electric mixer set at low speed, or with a spoon, beat batter until smooth and satiny. Add remaining flour gradually, changing from mixer or spoon to hands as the dough becomes stiffer.

4. Turn dough onto floured board. Knead until elastic (tight-feeling), smooth and no longer sticky enough to adhere to board; or continue to knead in mixing bowl until all flour and dough are cleaned from sides of bowl by kneading process.

5. Grease bowl and return dough to it; brush surface with melted butter or shortening. Cover with damp cloth, leaving edges outside bowl. Let rise in warm place (about 80°F.) until doubled in bulk.

6. Punch down dough and work the edges to center. Turn bottom side up and knead very lightly. Grease lightly, re-cover with damp cloth, and let rise again until almost doubled in bulk.

7. Preheat oven to 350°F. Grease two 9 x 5 x 3-inch loaf pans.

8. Punch down dough, knead lightly and divide into two equal parts. Shape into loaves. Place in prepared pans. Brush tops with melted butter or shortening. Re-cover with damp cloth. Let rise until center of dough is well rounded above pan, or until just doubled in bulk.

9. Bake for 1 hour, or until loaf shrinks from pan sides.

Brioches

About 18 brioches
The balance of eggs, liquid and flour overcomes the dryness in the atmosphere at high elevations.

1 package active dry yeast *or*
1 fresh cake compressed
yeast
¾ cup lukewarm water *or*
¼ cup lukewarm water
and ½ cup scalded milk,
cooled
4 cups sifted all-purpose
flour

3 eggs
1 egg, separated
½ teaspoon lemon extract *or*
1 teaspoon grated lemon
rind
⅔ cup softened butter
½ cup sugar
1 teaspoon salt

1. In large mixing bowl, sprinkle dry yeast or crumble cake yeast into lukewarm water, or into water and milk mixture. Stir to dissolve. Add 1 cup flour.
2. With electric mixer set at low speed, beat until smooth. Add 3 eggs and 1 egg yolk, one at a time, beating well between additions. Add lemon extract or rind, butter, sugar, salt and 1 cup flour. Beat 10 minutes at medium speed. Blend in remaining flour, mixing until smooth.
3. Scrape dough from sides of bowl. Cover with damp cloth, leaving edges on outside bowl. Let rise until doubled in bulk.
4. Stir down dough. Cover with waxed paper and re-cover with damp cloth. Refrigerate overnight, or for 12 hours.
5. Preheat oven to 375°F. Grease well a muffin pan with 3-inch cups.
6. Divide dough into two parts, one part to be two-thirds of the dough, the other to be one-third. Divide the larger

piece into 18 equal parts; roll each into a ball and place in a prepared muffin cup. Make a thumb print in top of each. Divide remaining dough into 18 small balls, and place one on top of each brioche. Brush tops with remaining egg white beaten lightly with 1 tablespoon water. Cover with damp cloth. Let rise until just doubled in bulk.

7. Bake 15 to 20 minutes, or until rolls shrink from muffin cup sides and are golden brown.

Croissants

40 croissants

1 package active dry yeast *or* 1 cake compressed fresh yeast
¼ cup lukewarm water
1 cup ice-cold milk
1 cold egg

¾ teaspoon salt
1 tablespoon sugar
3½ cups sifted all-purpose flour
1 cup cold butter

1. In bowl large enough to accommodate raised dough, sprinkle dry yeast or crumble cake yeast into lukewarm water. Let stand 5 minutes.
2. Mix together milk, egg, salt and sugar. Add to yeast mixture.
3. Stir flour into yeast mixture. Knead dough in bowl, or on lightly floured pastry cloth or board, until smooth and elastic. Cover dough with damp cloth, leaving edges outside bowl. Let rise until doubled in bulk, then refrigerate until thoroughly chilled.

4. On very lightly floured board, roll out dough into 10- by 20-inch rectangle about ¼ inch thick. Dot half the dough with butter, leaving a half-inch rim around dough edge. Fold other half of dough over butter. With rolling pin, roll out dough into rectangle. Fold dough into thirds and turn around with narrow end toward you. Roll out again, fold and turn as before and roll out again. Fold again, wrap in waxed paper and refrigerate for 2 or more hours.

5. Roll out dough into 10- by 20-inch rectangle. Cut dough in half lengthwise and cut each strip crosswise into 10 pieces. Cut each piece diagonally, making 40 triangles. Beginning with the wide side, roll up each triangular piece, stretching it slightly; shape into a crescent. Place with points underneath, about 1½ inches apart on greased cookie sheets.

6. Cover with damp cloth. Let rise for 2 hours or until almost doubled in bulk, in cool room or refrigerator.

7. Preheat oven to 400°F. Bake 15 to 20 minutes, or until golden brown.

Kolatchen
(Sour-Cream Sweet Yeast Rolls)   2 to 3 dozen rolls

1 package active dry yeast *or*
1 fresh cake compressed yeast
¼ cup lukewarm water
1 cup scalded dairy sour cream
2 tablespoons melted shortening
¼ cup sugar

½ teaspoon salt
⅛ teaspoon baking soda
1 egg, beaten
3 cups sifted all-purpose flour
Melted butter
Cinnamon Nut Filling, page 255

1. Preheat oven to 375°F. Grease cookie sheet.
2. In bowl large enough to accommodate raised dough, sprinkle dry yeast or crumble cake yeast into lukewarm water. Stir to dissolve.
3. Into scalded cream stir shortening, sugar, salt and soda. Cool to lukewarm. Add to yeast mixture.
4. Add beaten egg. Mix well. Add one third of sifted flour. With a spoon, or electric mixer set at low speed, beat batter until smooth and satiny. Add remaining flour gradually, changing from mixer or spoon to hands, if necessary, as dough becomes stiffer.
5. Turn dough onto floured board and knead for a few minutes. Cover with damp cloth for 5 minutes.
6. Roll out dough ¼ inch thick. Brush generously with melted butter. Spread with Cinnamon Nut Filling. Cut into 3-inch squares. Roll squares up like small jelly rolls. Place on prepared cookie sheet, seams down.
7. Bake 15 to 20 minutes, or until golden brown.

Apricot Sour-Cream Rolls: In Step 6, substitute 1 can (12 ounces) apricot cake and pastry filling for Cinnamon Nut Filling.

Cheese Straws

About 2 dozen

2 tablespoons butter
1 cup grated New York sharp cheese (Cheddar-type)
1 cup sifted all-purpose flour

1 teaspoon double-acting baking powder
½ teaspoon salt
¼ teaspoon paprika
6 to 7 tablespoons cold water

1. Preheat oven to 400°F. Grease cookie sheet.
2. In mixing bowl, mix butter and cheese together.
3. Mix and sift flour, baking powder, salt and paprika together. Combine dry ingredients with cheese mixture.
4. Add just enough cold water to make an easily rolled dough. Knead lightly.
5. On well-floured board, roll out dough ⅛ inch thick.
6. Cut into strips ½ inch wide and 4 inches long. Place on greased cookie sheet.
7. Bake about 5 minutes, or until golden. Cool on rack.

Stollen
(German Christmas Coffee Cake)   2 loaves

½ cup citron *or*
    ½ cup candied mixed
    fruits
2 tablespoons rum
2 packages active dry
    yeast *or* 2 fresh cakes
    compressed yeast
1½ cups scalded milk,
    cooled to room
    temperature
6 cups sifted all-purpose
    flour
¾ teaspoon salt

¾ cup sugar
1½ cups softened butter
2 eggs, beaten
1 cup white raisins
1 cup finely chopped
    almonds
¾ teaspoon grated lemon
    rind
½ vanilla bean, finely
    chopped or grated, *or*
    ¾ teaspoon nutmeg or
    mace

1. Soak citron or candied mixed fruits in rum overnight.
2. Have all ingredients at room temperature.

3. In mixing bowl large enough to accommodate raised dough, sprinkle dry yeast or crumble cake yeast into cooled scalded milk. Stir until dissolved. Add enough flour to make a sponge. Cover bowl with damp cloth, leaving edges outside of bowl. Let rise until doubled in bulk.

4. Stir down sponge with electric mixer set at low speed or with spoon. Add salt, sugar, 1¼ cups softened butter and beaten eggs. Beat well. Gradually add remaining flour, changing from mixer or spoon to hands, if necessary, as dough becomes stiffer. Mix in raisins, almonds, lemon rind and chopped vanilla bean (or nutmeg or mace). Continue to mix until fruits and nuts are well distributed.

5. Turn dough onto floured board and knead until smooth and elastic. Divide dough in half and shape each half into a ball. Roll or pat each ball into an oval 10 inches long, or roll or pat all of dough into a large oval.

6. Melt remaining ¼ cup butter. Brush onto dough, reserving 2 tablespoons. Fold dough over lengthwise, not quite in half (like a Parker House roll). Pinch ends together. Brush with remaining melted butter.

7. Grease cookie or baking sheet. Place Stollen on prepared pan and cover with damp cloth. Let rise until nearly doubled in bulk. Meanwhile, preheat oven to 375°F.

8. Brush Stollen with butter. Bake small loaves about 30 minutes; large loaf about 45 to 50 minutes or until golden brown. At end of baking period, brush with melted butter and sprinkle with granulated sugar or glaze with powdered sugar mixed with a little milk (coating should be quite thick).

9. Wrap well to store; Stollen keeps well if not allowed to dry out.

Cranberry Orange Bread

1 loaf

1 egg, beaten	4 teaspoons double-acting
2 tablespoons melted butter	baking powder
1 cup milk	½ cup sugar
3 cups sifted all-purpose	Grated rind of 1 orange
flour	½ cup chopped nutmeats
1 teaspoon salt	1 cup chopped cranberries

1. Preheat oven to 350°F. Grease a 9 x 5 x 3-inch loaf pan.
2. In mixing bowl, blend beaten egg, melted butter and milk.
3. Mix and sift flour, salt, baking powder and ¼ cup sugar together. Add grated orange rind and nutmeats.
4. Combine dry ingredients with liquid mixture, stirring only until blended.
5. Mix remaining ¼ cup sugar with chopped cranberries. Fold into batter.
6. Pour batter into prepared pan.
7. Bake about 1 hour, or until toothpick inserted in center comes out clean. Bread will slice best if cooled overnight.

Irish Buttermilk Bread

(Irish Cake)   2 loaves

4 cups sifted all-purpose	¼ cup butter *or* margarine
flour	1 teaspoon baking soda
2 tablespoons sugar	2 cups buttermilk
1 teaspoon salt	2 cups seedless raisins
¾ teaspoon double-acting	Cream
baking powder	

1. Preheat oven to 375°F. Generously grease two 9-inch pie plates.
2. Into mixing bowl, mix and sift flour, sugar, salt and baking powder.
3. With two table knives or pastry blender, cut butter or margarine into flour mixture until it is the consistency of coarse corn meal.
4. Dissolve soda in buttermilk. Add to dry ingredients, stirring until all ingredients are moistened. (Dough will be soft.) Add raisins.
5. On lightly floured board, knead dough until somewhat smooth, about 15 to 20 strokes. Divide dough in half. Shape each half into a round loaf that will fit closely into pie plate.
6. Place each loaf in prepared pan. Brush with cream. Cut a cross in top of loaf to keep it from cracking.
7. Bake 45 minutes, or until toothpick inserted in center comes out clean. Remove from pans and cool on wire rack.

Jalapeño Spoon Bread
About 10 servings

3 cups corn-bread mix
2½ cups milk
½ cup cooking oil
3 eggs, beaten
3 tablespoons sugar
1 large onion, grated

1 can (8¾ ounces) cream-style corn
1 can (4 ounces) Jalapeño peppers (green chilis), finely chopped
1½ cups grated natural Cheddar cheese

1. Preheat oven to 375°F. Grease a 12 x 8 x 2-inch pan.
2. Put corn-bread mix into large mixing bowl.
3. In medium-size mixing bowl, combine remaining ingredients. Mix well.
4. Quickly combine liquid mixture with corn-bread mix. Pour into prepared pan.
5. Bake 35 to 45 minutes, or until knife inserted in center comes out clean.
6. Serve hot.

Sour-Cream Coffee Cake

About 16 servings
The balance of basic ingredients and the use of sour cream produce a reliably moist result in this coffee cake.

½ cup softened butter	2 cups sifted cake flour
½ cup shortening	½ teaspoon salt
1¼ cups sugar	1 teaspoon double-acting
2 eggs	baking powder
½ teaspoon baking soda	1 teaspoon vanilla extract
1 cup dairy sour cream	Streusel Topping, page 255

1. Preheat oven to 350°F. Grease and flour 10 x 4-inch tube pan.
2. Cream butter and shortening with sugar until light and fluffy. Add eggs one at a time, beating well after each addition.
3. Dissolve soda in sour cream.
4. Mix and sift flour, salt and baking powder together.
5. Add dry ingredients alternately with sour cream to the creamed mixture, mixing well after each addition. Add vanilla extract. Mix well.

6. Pour batter into prepared pan. Sprinkle with Streusel Topping.
7. Bake 1 hour, or until cake center springs back when pressed with fingertip.

Orange Muffins

12 muffins

1 egg
¼ cup sugar
3 tablespoons melted butter
  or shortening
1¼ cups milk
2¼ cups sifted all-purpose
  flour

4 teaspoons double-acting
  baking powder
¾ teaspoon salt
Pulp and grated rind of
  1 orange

1. Preheat oven to 425°F. Grease and flour muffin pan with 3-inch cups.
2. In mixing bowl, beat egg. Blend in sugar, melted butter or shortening and milk.
3. Into larger mixing bowl mix and sift together flour, baking powder and salt.
4. Make a well in center of dry ingredients. Add small amount of liquid mixture. Blend quickly. Add remaining liquid mixture, using as few strokes as possible to blend the two together. Fold in orange pulp and rind.
5. Fill prepared muffin cups two-thirds full.
6. Bake 25 to 30 minutes, or until center springs back when lightly pressed with fingertips and muffins shrink from muffin cup sides.

Date Muffins with Streusel Topping

12 to 15 muffins

⅓ cup shortening
½ cup sugar
1 egg
¾ cup milk
2 cups sifted all-purpose
  flour
½ teaspoon salt

¼ teaspoon fresh cream
  of tartar
2 teaspoons double-acting
  baking powder
1 cup chopped dates
Streusel Topping, page 255

1. Preheat oven to 350°F. Grease muffin pan with 2½ inch cups.
2. Cream shortening with sugar until light and fluffy. Beat in egg. Add milk. Beat well.
3. Mix and sift flour, salt, cream of tartar and baking powder together.
4. Add dry ingredients to creamed mixture a little at a time, mixing thoroughly after each addition. Stir in dates.
5. Sprinkle a generous teaspoonful of Streusel Topping into prepared muffin cups. Pour in batter, filling cups two-thirds full.
6. Sprinkle additional teaspoonful of Streusel Topping over batter.
7. Bake 20 to 25 minutes, or until toothpick inserted in center comes out clean and muffins shrink from muffin cup sides.

DOUGHNUTS, CRULLERS AND FRITTERS

Pecan Doughnuts

3 dozen

Doughnuts made from sea-level recipes are frequently cracked, absorb too much fat, and have a hard brown crust. These recipes have the correct balance of leavening, fat, and sugar to avoid these characteristics.

1 cup sugar	1 teaspoon salt
3 eggs	¼ teaspoon ground
2½ tablespoons melted butter	cinnamon
¼ cup milk	¼ teaspoon ground nutmeg
3½ cups sifted all-purpose	½ cup chopped pecans
flour	Powdered sugar
4 teaspoons double-acting	
baking powder	

1. In mixing bowl, beat eggs well and gradually add sugar. Beat in melted butter and milk.
2. Mix and sift flour, baking powder, salt, cinnamon and nutmeg together.
3. Add dry ingredients to liquid mixture. Stir until blended. Add pecans.
4. Dough may be chilled until manageable, if necessary.
5. In large saucepan or deep-fat fryer, heat cooking oil or shortening to 350° to 360°F. Have sufficient fat to float doughnuts—it should be at least 1½ inches deep.
6. On well-floured surface, roll out dough ⅜ inch thick. Cut with doughnut cutter. If cut-out doughnuts are dried for 15 minutes before frying, they will absorb less fat.

7. Drop doughnuts into preheated fat. Brown on one side. Turn and brown on other, about 3 to 5 minutes in all. Drain on paper toweling.
8. Roll in powdered sugar, or sprinkle with mixture of 2 teaspoons cinnamon and ⅔ cup granulated sugar. Doughnuts may be shaken in paper bag containing either sugar coating.

French Market Crullers

About 2½ dozen

At higher altitudes, the lower boiling point of water in foods requires lowering of temperatures for deep-fat frying. Use shortening or oil heated to 350° to 360°F.

⅔ cup sugar	3½ cups sifted all-purpose
4 eggs, beaten	flour
⅓ cup melted shortening	3 teaspoons double-acting
⅓ cup milk	baking powder
¾ teaspoon grated lemon	¼ teaspoon salt
rind	Shortening or cooking oil
	Powdered sugar

1. In large mixing bowl, gradually add sugar to beaten eggs. Blend in melted shortening, milk and lemon rind.
2. Mix and sift flour, baking powder and salt together.
3. Add dry ingredients to liquid mixture, stirring until blended.
4. Chill dough until manageable.
5. In large saucepan or deep-fat fryer, heat cooking oil or shortening to 350°-360°F. Have sufficient oil or shortening to float crullers—it should be at least 1½ inches deep.

6. On well-floured board, roll out dough ¼ inch thick. Cut into strips 8 inches long. Fold in half lengthwise, twist several times and pinch ends together; or form into knots.
7. Fry a few at a time until golden brown on all sides, 3½ minutes on the first side, 2½ minutes on the second side.
8. Serve hot or cold, dusted with powdered sugar.

Fruit or Berry Fritters

4 to 6 servings
Using too-hot cooking fat will result in a disappointingly overbrowned fritter with an underdone middle. A thermometer will help to keep cooking oil or shortening properly heated to 350° to 360°F.

2 eggs, separated
1 tablespoon melted butter
½ cup milk or juice from fruit to be used
1 to 1½ cups sifted all-purpose flour
¼ teaspoon salt
2 teaspoons double-acting baking powder

1½ tablespoons sugar
1½ to 2 cups of fresh or frozen (thawed) fruit *or* berries of your choice, well drained and sliced if large
Powdered sugar

1. In mixing bowl, beat egg yolks. Blend in butter and milk or fruit juice.
2. Mix and sift flour, salt, baking powder and sugar together.
3. Blend dry ingredients with liquid mixture. Stir well. Let batter rest for 2 or more hours, covered and refrigerated.
4. In large saucepan or deep-fat fryer, heat cooking oil or shortening to 350° to 360°F. Have sufficient fat to float fritters—it should be at least 1½ inches deep.

5. Beat batter until smooth. Beat egg whites until stiff; with rubber spatula or flat whisk, fold into batter.
6. Dip fruit pieces in or sprinkle berries with powdered sugar, then dip sugar-coated fruit in batter, or mix berries or chopped fruit gently into batter.
7. Drop batter-covered fruit slices (or fruit-filled batter by spoonfuls into preheated cooking fat. Fry a few at a time until golden brown on all sides. Drain on paper toweling.
8. Serve hot. If desired, sprinkle with additional sugar.

Blueberry Pancakes

Serves 4

5 tablespoons sugar	2½ cups sifted all-purpose
3 eggs, beaten	flour
4 tablespoons melted butter	1 teaspoon salt
½ teaspoon vanilla extract,	1 teaspoon double-acting
if desired	baking powder
2 cups milk	¾ cup fresh or well-drained
	canned blueberries

1. Preheat very lightly greased griddle, skillet or electric skillet.
2. Add sugar to beaten eggs. Blend in melted butter, vanilla extract (if desired) and milk.
3. Into a pitcher or a mixing bowl that pours, mix and sift flour, salt and baking powder.
4. Make a well in center of dry ingredients. Add small amount of liquid mixture. Blend quickly. Add remaining liquid, using as few strokes as possible to blend in. Gently fold in blueberries.

5. When a few drops of water sprinkled on the hot cooking surface bounce and sputter, the temperature is right (about 400°F. on electric skillet).
6. Pour or spoon batter onto cooking surface, making cakes in size desired. When top of pancake is well covered with bubbles beginning to burst, turn pancake and bake until underside is done. Turn only once. Serve immediately.

Swedish Pancakes

Serves 4

Serve these superlative paper-thin pancakes with lingonberry syrup or with sour cream and lingonberries.

2 cups milk
½ cup all-purpose flour
½ teaspoon salt

2 tablespoons sugar
4 eggs

1. Preheat very lightly greased griddle, skillet or electric skillet.
2. In mixing bowl, beat milk, flour, salt and sugar together until smooth. Add eggs and beat again. Batter will be very thin.
3. When a few drops of water sprinkled on the hot cooking surface bounce and sputter, the temperature is right (about 400°F. on electric skillet) . Pour or spoon batter onto griddle in very small amounts.
4. When top of pancake is well covered with bubbles beginning to burst, turn pancake and bake until underside is done. Turn only once. Serve immediately.

Sour-Cream Waffles

Serves 4

3 eggs, separated (beat whites until stiff, but not dry)
1½ teaspoons sugar
2 cups dairy sour cream

1¼ cups sifted cake flour
⅛ teaspoon salt
2 teaspoons double-acting baking powder
1 teaspoon baking soda

1. Preheat waffle iron.
2. Beat egg yolks until thick and lemon-colored. Add sugar to beaten egg yolks. Blend in sour cream.
3. Into pitcher or mixing bowl that pours, mix and sift flour, salt, baking powder and soda.
4. Make a well in center of dry ingredients. Add small amount of liquid mixture. Blend quickly. Add remaining liquid, using as few strokes as possible to blend in.
5. With pliable rubber scraper or whisk, gently fold in stiffly beaten egg whites.
6. Fill waffle iron two-thirds full. Bake approximately 5 minutes, or until done as desired. Serve immediately.

Flavorful Additions to Waffles: Into basic batter fold any one of these:

¾ cup chopped ripe bananas
½ cup well-drained canned crushed pineapple
¾ cup fresh or well-drained canned blueberries
½ cup shredded coconut
1 cup well-drained canned whole kernel corn

½ cup cold cooked rice
1 cup chopped dates or figs
2 teaspoons grated orange rind
⅔ cup puréed apricots
¾ cup crisply cooked crumbled bacon

Buttered Bread Crumbs

1 cup

1 cup bread crumbs
3 to 4 tablespoons melted butter *or* margarine

In small skillet, sauté bread crumbs in melted butter or margarine.

Flavorful Additions to Buttered Bread Crumbs:

Grated cheese	Finely chopped parsley
Finely chopped onions	Curry powder
Paprika	Garlic powder

Popovers

Popovers made by sea-level recipes will expand too rapidly at altitudes over 2,500 feet thereby losing their steam before a crust can form: thus a stronger batter is needed at high elevations. This recipe is time-and-family-tested, and success depends on following it to the letter. Be sure to have the oven preheated to 450°F. and the pans well buttered. Do not peek during baking!

For 8 popovers:

2 large or 3 small eggs	1 cup sifted all-purpose flour
1 cup milk	½ teaspoon salt

For 16 popovers:

5 large eggs	2 cups sifted all-purpose flour
2 cups milk	1 teaspoon salt

1. Preheat oven to 450°F. Grease very generously and heat in oven either muffin pan (2½-inch cups), custard cups or popover pan.
2. In mixing bowl, beat eggs and combine with milk.
3. Mix and sift flour and salt together. Add dry ingredients to liquids. Beat well.
4. Pour batter into preheated and greased cups, filling them half full.
5. Bake at 450°F. for 15 minutes. *Reduce* temperature to 350°F. and bake 20 minutes more, being careful not to open oven door at any time.

Casseroles & Pasta
& Rice Dishes

Risotto

(Italian Rice) 4 servings

4 tablespoons butter
1 medium onion, chopped
1 small clove garlic,
  minced
1 cup uncooked rice,
  preferably a round-grain
  type

3 cups hot chicken broth *or*
  3 chicken bouillon cubes
  dissolved in 3 cups hot
  water
½ cup grated Parmesan or
  Romano cheese
Salt
Pepper

1. In large saucepan with cover, or Dutch oven, melt 3 tablespoons butter. Sauté onion in butter over medium heat
   until golden. Add garlic and rice. Stir until rice is golden,
   or about 4 minutes.
2. Add chicken broth or chicken bouillon cubes dissolved
   in hot water. Cover and cook over low heat about 25
   minutes, or until rice is tender and most of the liquid
   has been absorbed, stirring lightly with a fork occasionally. (Risotto should be of a creamy consistency when
   served, so it may be necessary to add a little additional
   boiling water during last few minutes of cooking.)

3. Remove from heat. Add remaining 1 tablespoon butter and ¼ cup grated cheese. Toss lightly with fork. Taste to determine if seasoning is correct. Turn into warmed serving dish. Sprinkle with remaining ¼ cup grated cheese. Serve immediately.

Risotto Milanese: Add ¼ teaspoon saffron with broth or water, and sauté ½ cup fresh, chopped mushrooms with rice in Step 1. In Step 2, substitute 1 cup dry sauterne or other dry white wine for 1 cup chicken broth or water.

Risotto with Sausage: Preheat oven to 350°F. In Step 1, sauté rice in butter as directed. Set aside. Brown ½ pound Italian sausage, cut into ½-inch slices in 1 tablespoon butter. Add ¼ cup chopped parsley, ⅛ teaspoon crumbled sage, and 1 can (6 ounces) tomato paste to sausage. In Step 2, substitute 3 cups water for chicken broth (or chicken bouillon cubes and water). Simmer for 1 hour. Add rice. Pour mixture into 2-quart casserole with cover. Bake, covered, 1 hour. 15 minutes before end of baking period, sprinkle with grated cheese. Return to oven, uncovered, to finish baking.

Risotto Alla Finanziera: Follow directions for Risotto. While it is cooking, make sauce: In skillet, melt 2 tablespoons butter. Add 1 medium onion, chopped, and sauté until limp. Add 1¼ cups sliced fresh mushrooms; ½ pound chicken livers, cut in bite-size pieces; ⅛ teaspoon each ground savory and garlic salt. Sauté about 6 minutes, turning livers to brown evenly. Add ¼ cup sherry or Madeira wine. Cook a few moments on high heat to reduce liquid to a few spoonfuls. Make well in center of Risotto. Spoon sauce into well. Sprinkle with Parmesan cheese.

Hominy and Almond Casserole

6 to 8 servings

1 can (10½ ounces) cream
  of mushroom soup
½ cup coffee cream
⅛ teaspoon cayenne pepper
1 teaspoon Worcestershire
  sauce
1 teaspoon celery seed
½ teaspoon pepper

1 teaspoon salt
1 can (No. 2½) hominy,
  drained
6 ounces almonds, blanched,
  toasted and cut in half
Buttered Bread Crumbs,
  page 75

1. Preheat oven to 350°F. Butter 2-quart casserole.
2. In small saucepan, combine soup, cream, cayenne pepper, Worcestershire sauce, celery seed, pepper and salt. Simmer over low heat for 6 minutes.
3. Place drained hominy in prepared casserole.
4. Add almonds to soup mixture. Pour over hominy. Sprinkle top with Buttered Bread Crumbs.
5. Bake about 45 minutes. Serve hot.

Tamale Soufflé

6 servings

1 medium onion, chopped
¼ cup olive oil
3 eggs, separated (beat
  whites until stiff, but not
  dry)

½ cup yellow corn meal
¼ cup milk
½ cup tomato sauce
2 teaspoons chili powder
¾ teaspoon salt

1. Preheat oven to 350°F. Butter a 1-quart ring mold.
2. In small skillet, sauté onion in 1 tablespoon olive oil until limp. Cool.
3. In mixing bowl, beat egg yolks slightly. Combine remaining olive oil, slightly beaten egg yolks, corn meal, milk, tomato sauce, chili powder, salt and sautéed onion.
4. With pliable rubber scraper or whisk, gently fold in stiffly beaten egg whites. Pour into prepared ring mold. Place mold in shallow pan on oven rack. Pour boiling water into pan to depth of 1 inch.
5. Bake 1 to 1¼ hours, or until silver knife inserted in center comes out clean. Remove from oven. Allow to set a few minutes.
6. Unmold onto hot platter and serve at once. If desired, fill center with creamed crab, lobster or other seafood.

Gnocchi

4 to 5 servings

2½ cups milk	1 egg, beaten
1 cup farina, cream of wheat or white cornmeal	¼ teaspoon salt
3 tablespoons butter	½ cup grated Parmesan cheese

1. Lightly grease 8 x 8 x 2-inch baking dish.
2. In medium-size saucepan, scald milk. Sprinkle farina, cream of wheat or cornmeal into milk. Cook, stirring constantly, about 10 minutes, or until thickened. Remove from heat and beat in butter, beaten egg and salt until smooth.

3. Spread in prepared pan. Refrigerate about 3 hours.
4. Preheat oven to 425°F. Generously grease a 9 x 9 x 2-inch baking dish.
5. Cut gnocchi into approximately 2-inch squares. Place squares in prepared dish, overlapping them slightly. Dot with remaining 2 tablespoons butter. Sprinkle with grated cheese.
6. Bake about 15 minutes, or until bubbly and cheese is melted. Serve immediately.

Gnocchi with Tomato Sauce: In Step 5, before sprinkling with cheese, pour 1 cup tomato sauce over squares.

Macaroni-Spinach Casserole

8 servings

4 cans (15 ounces each) macaroni and cheese
1 package (10 ounces) frozen chopped spinach, cooked and drained
½ pound natural sharp Cheddar cheese, grated
5 green onions and tops, chopped
1 can (2 ounces) pimiento, drained and chopped
½ teaspoon ground oregano
1 teaspoon salt
¼ teaspoon pepper

1. Preheat oven to 350°F. Grease 2-quart casserole.
2. In mixing bowl combine all ingredients, using only half of cheese.
3. Pour into prepared casserole. Sprinkle with remaining half of cheese.
4. Bake 1 hour, or until bubbly and browned.

Spanish Canalones

10 servings
This is an adaptation of a baked dish served in fine Spanish restaurants and homes.

2 pounds wide Italian lasagne-type noodles (discard any broken noodles)
Water
Salt
2 tablespoons olive or other cooking oil
¼ cup margarine
1 pound ground beef
1 pound ground veal
1 pound ground chicken livers
6 tablespoons all-purpose flour
¼ cup milk

1 large onion, finely chopped
1 clove garlic, crushed
3 ripe or drained canned tomatoes, chopped
2 tablespoons melted butter
Freshly ground pepper
3 bouillon cubes dissolved in ¼ cup of chicken broth or consommé
4 cans (10½ ounces each) cream of mushroom soup
½ cup grated Parmesan cheese
½ cup grated mozzarella cheese

1. Drop noodles into boiling water to which salt and 2 tablespoons oil have been added. Cook until almost done.
   Rinse, and lay in a single layer on paper toweling or a clean tea towel.
2. Preheat oven to 350°F. Butter a 13 x 9 x 2-inch baking dish.
3. In skillet, melt margarine. Sauté beef, veal and livers until meat changes color and is no longer raw. Sprinkle with flour; blend, then add milk. Stir to blend.
4. In separate skillet, sauté onions, garlic and tomatoes in melted butter until limp.

5. Combine meat and tomato mixtures. Add salt and pepper to taste. Cool enough to permit handling.
6. Cut each noodle strip into thirds. On each piece place about 1 tablespoon filling. Roll up and place rolls, seam side down, close together in baking dish.
7. Dissolve bouillon cubes in broth or consommé and mix with mushroom soup. Spoon sauce over tops of rolls. Sprinkle with cheeses.
8. Bake for 1 hour.

American Chow Mein Casserole

6 servings

1½ pounds lean ground beef
1 cup diced celery
1 large onion, chopped
1 green pepper, chopped, if desired
½ cup uncooked rice
1 can (10½ ounces) cream of mushroom soup

1 can (10½ ounces) cream of chicken *or* chicken-rice soup
1 ¾ cups water
3 tablespoons soy sauce
1 can (4 ounces) mushrooms and liquid, if desired
2 cups canned or packaged chow mein noodles

1. Preheat oven to 350°F. Have ready 2½-quart casserole.
2. In large skillet over medium heat brown meat with celery, onion and green pepper, if desired. Drain off excess fat. Add all remaining ingredients except chow mein noodles. Pour into casserole.
3. Bake for 1 hour. Cover top with noodles. Bake 30 minutes longer.

Beef Enchiladas

12 enchiladas

RED CHILI SAUCE

1 can (No. 2) tomato sauce
1 teaspoon chili powder
1 teaspoon salt
1 teaspoon monosodium
  glutamate
1 teaspoon paprika

½ teaspoon onion powder
2 teaspoons ground red
  pepper
1 teaspoon ground cumin
  (*cominos*)
1 cup water

In medium-size saucepan, combine all ingredients. Simmer over low heat for 45 minutes.

FILLING

2 pounds lean ground
  beef
¼ cup chopped onion
½ cup tomato purée
1 teaspoon ground cumin
  (*cominos*)
¼ teaspoon dried oregano

2 teaspoons monosodium
  glutamate
2 teaspoons salt
1 teaspoon chili powder
1 clove garlic, minced
1 teaspoon paprika
1 teaspoon pepper

ENCHILADAS AND TOPPING

12 corn tortillas, fresh,
  canned or frozen and
  thawed

1 cup grated longhorn or
  other Cheddar-type cheese
1 cup chopped green onions
  and tops

1. In large skillet, brown beef and onion over medium heat. Add tomato purée, cumin, oregano, monosodium gluta-

mate, salt, chili powder, garlic, paprika and pepper. Simmer over low heat for 25 minutes.

2. Preheat oven to 375°F. Have ready 13 x 9 x 2-inch casserole or oven-proof dish.

3. Place a large spoonful of meat mixture in center of each tortilla. Add 1 tablespoon each grated cheese and green onions. Roll up tortilla.

4. Place the filled tortillas in baking dish, seams down. Pour generous amount of Red Chili Sauce over top of tortillas. Sprinkle with remaining cheese and green onion.

5. Bake for 5 to 8 minutes, or until thoroughly heated and bubbly.

Tagliarini

8 servings

A little more water and time than noted on package directions are requisites for cooking pastas above 3,000 feet.

1 cup chopped onion

¾ cup chopped green pepper

2 cloves garlic, minced

2 tablespoons olive *or* other cooking oil

2 pounds lean ground beef

2 cups drained canned pear tomatoes, chopped

1½ cups drained canned kernel corn

¼ cup tomato paste

1 teaspoon dried oregano

2 teaspoons salt

1 teaspoon celery salt

½ teaspoon freshly ground pepper

½ teaspoon ground allspice

1 teaspoon monosodium glutamate

1 teaspoon dried sweet basil

3 sprigs parsley, chopped

1½ cups grated sharp Cheddar cheese

1 cup chopped ripe olives

1 package (1 pound) spaghetti, cooked, rinsed, and drained

1. In large skillet with cover, sauté onions, green pepper, and garlic in hot oil until limp. Add ground beef, stirring and chopping to separate granules as it browns. Add tomatoes, corn, tomato paste, oregano, salt, celery salt, pepper, allspice, monosodium glutamate, sweet basil and parsley. Cover and bring to boil. Reduce temperature. Simmer for 30 minutes.
2. Stir in grated cheese and chopped olives. Heat until flavors are blended and sauce is bubbly.
3. Serve over hot, cooked spaghetti.

Pasta with Clam Sauce

4 servings

¼ cup olive oil
  2 cloves garlic, peeled and
    sliced
  2 cans (7 ounces each)
    minced clams
½ teaspoon salt
¼ teaspoon pepper *or*
    seasoned pepper

2 tablespoons chopped
    parsley
Dash powdered oregano,
    if desired
½ pound spaghetti, fettucine
    or linguini, cooked,
    drained and kept hot
Grated Parmesan or Romano
    cheese, if desired

1. In blender, combine olive oil, garlic and clams. Blend over low speed 1 minute, *or* beat with electric mixer.
2. In 1-quart saucepan, combine blended clams, salt, pepper or seasoned pepper, parsley and oregano, if desired. Heat through, but do not boil.
3. Pour over hot, cooked spaghetti, fettucine or linguini.
4. Serve with or without grated cheese.

Spaghetti with Seafood

6 to 8 servings

1 package (12 ounces) spaghetti, cooked and drained
1 cup diced crab meat
1 cup small, peeled, deveined shrimp
1 tablespoon sliced shallots *or* green onions
3 tablespoons melted butter
Salt
Pepper
1 teaspoon monosodium glutamate
1½ cups dry white wine

2 ounces brandy, if desired
1 cup warm Thick White Sauce, page 155
1 teaspoon chili sauce *or* dash liquid hot pepper sauce
2 teaspoons Worcestershire sauce
Cooked crab leg pieces
1 tablespoon chopped chives
Juice of 1 lemon
Grated Parmesan cheese

1. Place cooked and drained spaghetti on heated platter. Keep warm.
2. In large heavy saucepan, sauté crabmeat, shrimp and shallots or green onion in melted butter, turning to brown all sides nicely, about 5 minutes. Add salt and pepper to taste, and monosodium glutamate.
3. Blend in wine and brandy, if desired. Heat to boiling, but do not allow to boil. Simmer until liquid is reduced to half and shrimp are tender.
4. To White Sauce, add chili sauce (or liquid hot pepper sauce) and Worcestershire sauce. Add to seafood, stirring to blend.
5. Pour over hot, drained spaghetti on a platter. Garnish with cooked crab leg pieces. Sprinkle with chives and lemon juice.
6. Pass Parmesan cheese when serving.

Egg & Cheese Dishes

Egg Croquettes

6 servings

6 hard-cooked eggs, peeled
  and finely chopped
¾ to 1 cup warm Thick
  White Sauce, page 155
½ teaspoon chopped chives
½ teaspoon chopped parsley
¼ teaspoon paprika
¼ teaspoon salt

Flour
  1 egg, beaten with
  1 tablespoon water
Bread crumbs
Oil for cooking
  1 can (8 ounces) tomato
  sauce

1. Mix chopped eggs with just enough White Sauce to hold together; mixture should not be runny. Add chives, parsley, paprika and salt. Cool.
2. Form cooled mixture into balls, using 1 tablespoon mixture for each.
3. Dip into flour, then in beaten egg and water, then in bread crumbs. Refrigerate 1 hour.
4. In large saucepan or deep-fat fryer, heat cooking oil to 350° to 360°F. Have sufficient oil to float croquettes—it should be at least 1½ inches deep.
5. Fry a few at a time until golden brown on all sides. Drain on paper toweling.
6. Serve hot, with heated tomato sauce.

Eggs in Potato Nests

6 servings

6 hot baked potatoes	1 egg yolk beaten with
3 tablespoons butter	1 tablespoon water
Hot milk	6 eggs
½ teaspoon salt	Paprika
⅛ teaspoon pepper	

1. Slice potato tops off lengthwise. Scoop out insides.
2. Beat pulp with butter and enough hot milk to be fluffy. Add salt and pepper. Refill potato shells three-fourths full, making a hollow in tops. Brush with beaten egg yolk. Brown under broiler 2 minutes.
3. Break an egg into each potato and sprinkle with paprika and any additional seasonings, if desired.
4. Bake at 350°F. 15 to 20 minutes, or until egg is done to individual taste.

Scotch Eggs

3 servings

1 pound ground beef	2 shallots, finely chopped
1 teaspoon Worcestershire sauce	½ teaspoon beefsteak sauce
Dash garlic powder	1 teaspoon chopped parsley
½ teaspoon salt	3 hard-cooked eggs, peeled
¼ teaspoon pepper *or* seasoned pepper	Flour
1 small onion, finely chopped	2 eggs, beaten with 1 cup milk
	Bread crumbs

1. In mixing bowl combine beef, Worcestershire sauce, garlic powder, salt, pepper, onion, shallots, beefsteak sauce and parsley. Toss lightly. Divide into 3 balls. Flatten each ball into thin patty.
2. Place one hard-cooked egg in center of each patty. Cover completely with meat mixture, shaping into egg form.
3. Roll coated egg in flour. Dip in mixture of eggs beaten with milk. Roll in bread crumbs.
4. Preheat cooking oil or shortening to 350° to 360°F.; it should be at least 1½ inches deep. Fry croquettes, turning to brown all sides. Serve whole, or split in half.

Quiche Lorraine

6 servings

10-inch unbaked pie shell	4 eggs, beaten
1 small onion, finely chopped	2 cups coffee cream
2 tablespoons butter	1 tablespoon melted butter
8 strips bacon, crisply cooked and crumbled	½ teaspoon ground nutmeg
½ pound Swiss cheese, grated	¼ teaspoon salt
	Dash cayenne pepper
	¼ teaspoon pepper

1. Preheat oven to 400°F. Have ready unbaked pie shell.
2. Sauté onion in 2 tablespoons butter until limp. Sprinkle crisply cooked and crumbled bacon and onions into unbaked pie shell.
3. Mix cheese, beaten eggs, cream, 1 tablespoon melted butter, nutmeg, salt, cayenne pepper and pepper together. Pour over bacon and onions.
4. Bake at 400°F. for 15 minutes, *reduce* temperature to 350°F. and bake 30 minutes more, or until knife inserted in center comes out clean. Cut in wedges and serve hot.

Shrimp Quiche: Reduce Swiss cheese to ½ cup. In Step 3, add ¼ cup grated Parmesan cheese, 1½ tablespoons sherry, and ¾ cup sliced, cooked shrimp.

Spinach Quiche: In Step 3, substitute 1 package (10 ounces) frozen cooked, drained and chopped spinach for 1 cup cream. Add 1 clove finely minced garlic, if desired.

Cheese Soufflé

4 servings
Ingredient adjustments have been made to make these soufflés successful at higher altitudes.

4 eggs, separated (beat whites until stiff, but not dry)	1 cup grated **Cheddar cheese**
	½ teaspoon salt
	½ teaspoon prepared mustard, if desired
¼ cup butter	⅛ teaspoon pepper
¼ cup all-purpose flour	
1 cup milk	

1. Preheat oven to 350°F. Butter 1½-quart soufflé dish. Dust lightly with flour and grated Parmesan cheese or fine bread crumbs.
2. Beat egg yolks until thick and lemon-colored. Set aside. In saucepan, melt butter. Stir in flour. Gradually add milk and cook 3 to 5 minutes, stirring constantly, until mixture is thickened. Add cheese, salt, mustard and pepper. Stir until cheese melts.
3. Add a little hot sauce slowly to beaten yolks, mixing thoroughly. Add remainder of sauce and mix.
4. Fold in stiffly beaten egg whites.

5. Pour or spoon mixture into prepared soufflé dish. Mixture should fill dish to top, or at least reach to within ½ inch of top. (This assures good volume and attractive browning.)
6. Set soufflé in shallow pan on oven rack. Pour boiling water into pan to depth of 1 inch.
7. Bake for 25 to 35 minutes, or until a knife inserted into soufflé halfway between center and outside edge comes out clean. Serve immediately.

Fish Soufflé: In Step 2, substitute 1 cup cooked, flaked fish for cheese.

Vegetable Soufflé: Substitute for or add to cheese 1 cup cooked, chopped vegetables—carrots, peas, celery, or another of your choice.

Fish & Shellfish

Court Bouillon for Fish

6 cups
*Poaching fish or shellfish in court bouillon is a great method
for high altitudes because of the liquid heat.*

1 tablespoon butter	6 peppercorns
1 large onion, chopped	2 whole cloves
1 large carrot, chopped	1 bay leaf
2 stalks celery, chopped	1 tablespoon chopped parsley
2 quarts water	2 tablespoons vinegar *or*
1 teaspoon salt	lemon juice

1. In skillet or saucepan large enough to accommodate all
   ingredients, melt butter. Sauté onion, carrot and celery
   until limp, about 10 minutes.
2. Add remaining ingredients. Cover tightly. Bring to boil.
   Reduce heat and simmer 30 minutes.
3. Strain before using. Court bouillon keeps for several days
   if refrigerated, but should be discarded after being used.

Fumet

(Fish Stock) 2 cups
More concentrated than a court bouillon, this is used for making sauces for fish and other seafood dishes.

1 pound fish trimmings (tails, bones and heads)	1 large onion, sliced
	1 carrot, chopped
3 cups water	¼ cup chopped celery
2 cups dry white wine	1 teaspoon salt
½ bay leaf	1 teaspoon powdered thyme

1. In 3-quart saucepan, combine all ingredients. Bring to boil.
2. Reduce heat. Simmer 30 minutes, or just until liquid is reduced about one half. Do not overcook.
3. Strain, cool and remove any fat before using.

High-Country Fish Batter

This zesty batter is great at high altitudes because it seals in the tenderness and moisture of freshly caught fish, fresh-frozen fish, or shellfish.

1 can (11 ounces) beer	1 tablespoon double-acting baking powder
1 teaspoon salt	
⅛ teaspoon curry powder, if desired	Cake flour

1. Combine all ingredients, using enough cake flour to make batter the thickness desired. Thin batter will make a crisper coating; thick batter will make a heavier coating.

2. Dip fish or shellfish in batter. Deep-fat fry in hot cooking oil or shortening, preheated to 350° to 360°F., or fry in heavy skillet in preheated shortening or oil about ⅛ inch in depth. Fish is done when golden brown on all sides. Cooking time varies with type and size of fish or shellfish.

Poached Fish

Tie fish fillets, steaks, chunks, or whole fish in cheesecloth or place on poaching rack or trivet. Lower into shallow pan filled with simmering Court Bouillon, page 93, or Fumet, page 94. Cover and simmer until fish is tender, about 10 minutes for fillets, steaks, or pieces; longer for whole fish depending on size and variety of fish. A variable rule of thumb for whole fish is ½ to 1 minute per ounce. Remove fish, allow broth to drain off, and remove cheesecloth. Serve hot with lemon and butter, tartar sauce, or other sauce of choice.

Baked Stuffed Fish

Allow ¾ pound per serving
Baking a whole fish with the head on helps to seal in juices at higher elevations. Serve baked fish as soon as taken from the oven, so it will not become soggy.

Preheat oven to 375°F. Use fish no smaller than 3 pounds. Have pocket made for stuffing. Rub inside with salt and pepper. Stuff two-thirds full with Herb Stuffing for Fish. page 168. Fasten opening closed with skewers or picks. Place fish on greased rack in open roasting pan. Brush with melted butter or margarine, sprinkle with salt and seasoned pepper. Bake, basting with pan juices, until fish is tender and flakes easily, about 12 to 20 minutes a pound for fish over 5 pounds, and about 1 to 2 minutes per ounce for smaller fish. Serve baked fish with Béarnaise Sauce, page 157 or Chablis Sauce, page 157.

Fish Baked, Broiled, or Barbecued in Foil

6 servings
The air-tight foil produces flaky, tender, moist results.

6 fillets, steaks, *or* whole small
   pan-dressed fish (about
   2 pounds)
6 sheets heavy aluminum
   foil
Salt
Seasoned pepper or pepper

Dried dill seed, parsley *or*
   rosemary, if desired
Butter
6 lemon or lime slices
6 to 12 tablespoons dry
   white wine

1. Preheat oven to 400°F., preheat broiler, or have charcoal at cooking temperature in barbecue grill.
2. Place each individual serving of fish on a sheet of foil. Sprinkle with salt, seasoned pepper or pepper and dill, parsley or rosemary, if desired. Dot generously with butter. Top with slice of lemon or lime. Pour 1 to 2 tablespoons wine over fish. Fold foil up around fish and seal by folding, allowing a little space on top of fish.
3. Bake 20 to 30 minutes in oven, or for 15 minutes in broiler, or for 30 minutes over glowing charcoal. Fish will be tender and flake easily when done.

Baked Fillet of Halibut
4 servings

Cooking oil

4 halibut fillets (about
8 ounces each), 1½ inches
thick

All-purpose flour

Salt

Paprika

Tartar sauce, if desired

1. Preheat oven to 350°F. Pour 1 inch of cooking oil into flat baking dish.
2. Dredge fillets in flour. Place in baking dish, turning to coat both sides with oil. Sprinkle with salt and paprika to taste.
3. Bake for 25 to 30 minutes, or until fish is tender and flakes easily. Do not overbake, as it will make fish dry and tough.
4. Serve with tartar sauce, if desired.

Fillet of Sole or Flounder Romano
4 servings

4 fillets (about 1½ pounds)
of fresh or frozen and
thawed sole *or* flounder

3 tablespoons butter

1 can (6 ounces) small
deveined shrimp, drained

1 can (4½ ounces) chopped
ripe olives

1 can (4 ounces) mushroom
slices, drained

Romano Cheese Sauce,
page 156

Paprika

1. Preheat broiler. Butter flat baking dish large enough to hold fish in one layer.

2. In skillet, sauté sole or flounder in butter until lightly browned but not cooked through. Place in baking dish. Top each fillet with 2 or 3 shrimp, 1 teaspoon chopped olives, and one fourth of the mushroom slices. Cover with Romano Cheese Sauce. Sprinkle with paprika.
3. Broil until top is golden brown and fish is well heated through. Fish flakes easily when done. Do not overcook.

Broiled Fish with Soufflé Topping

6 servings

6 fish fillets, fresh *or* fresh-frozen and thawed (about 2 pounds)
Cooking oil or butter
½ cup mayonnaise
1 tablespoon finely chopped chives
2 tablespoons sweet pickle relish
1 tablespoon finely chopped parsley
1 tablespoon lemon juice
¼ teaspoon seasoned salt
¼ teaspoon paprika
¼ teaspoon powdered thyme
2 egg whites, beaten until stiff but not dry
Pimiento slices *or* sprigs of watercress

1. Preheat broiler. Grease shallow baking pan.
2. Wipe fillets with damp cloth and brush lightly with oil or softened butter. Place in baking pan.
3. Broil fish until it flakes easily, about 8 minutes. Remove from broiler.
4. Meanwhile, blend together mayonnaise, chives, relish, parsley, lemon juice, seasoned salt, paprika and thyme. Fold in stiffly beaten egg whites.
5. Drain pan juices from fish. Spread topping evenly over fish fillets.

6. Broil until golden brown, about 2 minutes. Garnish with pimiento slices or watercress sprigs.

Frogs' Legs Provençale
6 servings

36 (18 pairs) frogs' legs, skinned and with feet removed
½ teaspoon salt
⅛ teaspoon pepper
Flour
¼ to ½ cup butter
2 shallots, finely chopped

1 tablespoon parsley
2 tablespoons chopped fresh tomatoes
1 small clove garlic, finely chopped
Juice of 1 lemon
½ cup dry white wine

1. Wash frogs' legs and pat dry. Sprinkle with salt and pepper. Dust lightly with flour.
2. In large skillet, melt butter. Quickly sauté frogs' legs, turning to brown evenly, about 8 to 10 minutes. Remove to heated platter. To butter in pan add shallots, parsley, tomato and garlic. Blend well. Simmer 1 to 2 minutes. Add lemon juice and wine. Simmer few minutes more. Pour sauce over frogs' legs and serve immediately.

Red Snapper Caribbean
6 servings

½ cup butter
6 fillets of red snapper (about 2 pounds)

Juice of 2 limes
2 bananas
½ cup shredded coconut

1. Preheat oven to 450°F. Melt butter in flat baking dish large enough to hold fish in one layer.
2. Place fillets in dish, turning to coat both sides with butter.
3. Bake 5 minutes. Remove from oven and turn.
4. Mix in blender or mash together with a fork the lime juice, bananas and coconut, making a purée. Top fish with mixture (it will be quite thick).
5. Return fish to oven. Bake 4 to 5 minutes longer. Place under broiler to brown.

Tuna or Salmon Noodle Casserole
6 servings

2 cups Thick White Sauce (page 155)
8 ounces pimiento-flavored process cheese
3 cups cooked and drained noodles
1 can (7 ounces) tuna or salmon, drained and flaked

¾ pound fresh mushrooms, washed, dried and sliced
½ cup chopped pimiento
½ cup chopped green pepper
2 hard-cooked eggs, chopped
⅔ cup sliced stuffed green olives

1. Preheat oven to 375°F. Grease 2-quart casserole.
2. In 2-quart saucepan over low heat, warm cream sauce with cheese until cheese melts. Add remaining ingredients. Mix gently but thoroughly. Pour into prepared casserole.
3. Bake 1 hour, or until browned and bubbly.

Crab Veronica

6 servings

The French have a way of combining poultry or seafood with grapes, indicating this style of preparation by the term Véronique *(Veronica). It is quite special.*

1½ cups hot chicken consommé *or* chicken broth
3 to 4 cups cooked rice
½ cup chopped celery
¼ cup chopped parsley
4 tablespoons butter *or* margarine
4 tablespoons all-purpose flour
½ teaspoon salt

1 can (14½ ounces) evaporated milk
1 cup apple juice
1 tablespoon lemon juice
2 cans (7 ounces each) crabmeat *or* 1 pound fresh crabmeat
1 cup green grapes, seeded if necessary
Lemon slices

1. Preheat oven to 375°F. Butter 6 individual ramekins.
2. In medium-size saucepan, pour hot consommé or broth over rice. Stir in celery and parsley. Over medium heat, simmer rice mixture until celery is tender. Set aside.
3. Drain canned crabmeat, flake, and remove bony tissue, or flake fresh crabmeat.
4. In medium-size saucepan, melt butter. Stir in flour and salt. Add milk. Cook, stirring constantly, until sauce is thickened. Boil 1 minute. Remove from heat. Stir in apple and lemon juices until blended. Fold in crabmeat and grapes.
5. Divide rice mixture into ramekins. Spoon one-sixth crab mixture into each.
6. Bake until heated through and bubbly—about 20 minutes. Garnish with lemon slices.

Lobster and Tenderloin Kebabs

6 servings

1½ pounds lobster meat, cut
    in 1½-inch cubes
1½ pounds beef tenderloin,
    cut in 1½-inch cubes
  ¾ cup grated Parmesan
    cheese

2 eggs, beaten with
  2 tablespoons water
1 cup fine bread crumbs
12 large mushrooms, washed
   and dried
12 pineapple chunks

1. Preheat broiler. Have broiler pan ready.
2. Roll lobster and beef cubes in Parmesan cheese. Dip in egg wash. Roll lightly in bread crumbs.
3. Thread skewers with a piece of lobster, a mushroom, a beef cube and a pineapple chunk, repeating if there is room.
4. Broil until desired doneness.

Hot Crab or Shrimp Soufflé

10 servings

10 slices bread
  2 cups cooked and flaked
    crabmeat *or* cooked,
    peeled and deveined
    shrimp, cut in ½-inch
    pieces
  ½ cup mayonnaise
  1 green pepper, seeded and
    chopped

1 cup chopped celery
1 small onion, chopped
3 cups milk
4 eggs, beaten
1 can (10½ ounces) cream
  of mushroom soup
½ cup grated Cheddar cheese
Paprika

1. Butter a 13 x 9 x 2-inch baking dish.
2. Dice 4 slices of bread. Place in baking dish.
3. Mix crab or shrimp, mayonnaise, green pepper, celery and onion. Spread over bread cubes.
4. Trim crusts from remaining slices of bread. Place trimmed slices closely together on top of shellfish.
5. Mix milk with beaten eggs. Pour over bread slices. Cover with foil or plastic wrap. Refrigerate overnight.
6. When ready to serve, uncover and bake in oven preheated to 325°F. for 15 minutes. Remove from oven. Pour soup over top, then sprinkle with grated cheese and paprika. Bake 1 hour longer.

Neptune Casserole

4 servings

½ pound cooked lobster
½ pound cooked, peeled and deveined shrimp
½ pound cooked crabmeat
2 teaspoons finely chopped onion
2 cups milk
½ cup cream
8 teaspoons butter
4 tablespoons all-purpose flour

3 tablespoons dry sauterne
⅛ teaspoon powdered thyme
¼ teaspoon salt
⅛ teaspoon pepper
1 tablespoon grated Parmesan cheese
1 tablespoon grated American cheese
Paprika

1. Cut seafood into ½-inch pieces.
2. In saucepan, simmer onions with milk and cream over low heat.

3. Make roux: In separate saucepan, melt butter. Stir in flour. Cook about 5 minutes, stirring continuously (roux must not brown). Strain heated milk into roux. Stir until blended. Cook a few minutes until smooth and thickened. Add wine, thyme, salt, pepper and half the cheeses. Add seafood.
4. Spoon mixture into 2-quart buttered casserole. Sprinkle with remaining cheese and paprika.
5. Bake at 350°F. until heated through. Place under broiler to brown top.

Deviled Oysters

8 servings

1 medium onion, finely chopped	2 tablespoons Worcestershire sauce
½ cup butter	½ teaspoon pepper
1 quart oysters, well drained and cut in pieces	¼ teaspoon cayenne pepper
3 eggs, beaten	½ teaspoon paprika
4 tablespoons lemon juice	Few drops liquid hot pepper sauce
3 cups soda cracker crumbs	1 teaspoon salt

1. Preheat oven to 400°F. Butter 8 individual seafood shells or ramekins or 2-quart casserole.
2. In small skillet, sauté onion in butter until limp. Cool.
3. In large mixing bowl, combine oysters and beaten eggs. Add onions and remaining ingredients. Mix well. Spoon into prepared shells, ramekins or casserole.
4. Bake shells or ramekins about 20 to 25 minutes, casserole about 45 minutes.

Coquilles St. Jacques

6 to 8 servings

½ cup dry sherry
1½ pounds scallops, washed, drained and cut in ½-inch cubes
1 small onion, chopped
7 tablespoons melted butter
¼ cup all-purpose flour
½ cup milk
1 cup cream

1 tablespoon chopped parsley
½ pound fresh mushrooms, washed, dried and sliced
1 tablespoon Worcestershire sauce
Dash pepper
½ cup cornflake crumbs
Grated Parmesan cheese

1. Preheat oven to 350°F. Butter 6 to 8 individual ramekins or seafood shells, or 2-quart casserole.
2. Pour ¼ cup sherry over drained scallops.
3. In small skillet, sauté chopped onion in 4 tablespoons melted butter until limp, about 5 minutes. Add flour, stirring to blend. Gradually add milk and cream. Heat, but *do not* boil, stirring constantly until thickened. Remove from heat.
4. In separate saucepan, sauté parsley and mushrooms in remaining 3 tablespoons butter, until golden brown, about 5 minutes. Do not overcook. Add Worcestershire sauce, pepper and remaining ¼ cup sherry. Combine with scallops, mushrooms and cream sauce.
5. Spoon into ramekins, shells or casserole. Sprinkle top with cornflake crumbs and grated cheese. If shells are used, place on cookie sheet.
6. Bake until mixture is bubbly and tops are brown—about 20 minutes for individual servings or 35 minutes for a casserole.

Shrimp Tempura

(Butterfly Shrimp)   About 2 dozen

1½ pounds large shrimp,
   peeled and deveined
Salt
   1 cup milk, water or beer

½ teaspoon monosodium
   glutamate
1 cup all-purpose flour
Cooking oil
Tempura Sauce, page 162

1. Preheat cooking oil to 350° to 360°F.
2. Split shrimp down the back to within ½ inch of the tail.
   Press out flat like a butterfly. Sprinkle with salt.
3. Beat together milk, water or beer, and monosodium glutamate. Stir in flour very lightly; do not overmix.
4. Dip shrimp into batter. Drop one by one into heated cooking oil. Fry until golden, about 3 minutes. Serve hot with
   Tempura Sauce or chutney.

Shrimp de Jonghe

8 servings

2 pounds shrimp, cooked,
   peeled and deveined
1 cup butter
4 cloves garlic, skewered on
   a toothpick
¼ teaspoon dried tarragon
½ teaspoon chopped parsley
½ teaspoon chopped shallots

Dash ground nutmeg
Dash ground mace
Dash ground thyme
Dash liquid hot pepper sauce
   1 teaspoon salt
⅛ teaspoon pepper
½ cup dry sauterne *or* sherry
1 cup fine dry bread crumbs

1. Preheat oven to 400°F. Divide shrimp among 8 buttered ramekins.
2. In small heavy saucepan, melt ¾ cup butter. Sauté garlic, tarragon, parsley and shallots just until moistened and slightly browned. Add nutmeg, mace, thyme, liquid hot pepper sauce, salt, pepper and wine. Heat, but do not boil. Remove garlic.
3. Pour sauce over shrimp. Sprinkle top with bread crumbs. Drizzle remaining ¼ cup butter over bread crumbs.
4. Bake 10 to 15 minutes, or until heated through and nicely browned.

Shrimp Fromage

6 to 8 servings

¾ cup butter
1 clove garlic, minced
1 cup fresh *or* canned sliced mushrooms, drained
3 shallots, chopped
¼ cup all-purpose flour
½ teaspoon salt
¼ teaspoon thyme
⅛ teaspoon pepper
½ teaspoon monosodium glutamate
2 cups milk
4 ounces grated Cheddar cheese
4 ounces grated Swiss cheese
2 ounces grated mozzarella cheese
2 tablespoons grated Parmesan cheese
½ cup creamed cottage cheese
½ cup dairy sour cream
¼ cup dry white wine
1 package (10 ounces) macaroni, cooked and drained
2 pounds cooked, deveined shrimp, cut in half
¼ cup bread crumbs

1. Preheat oven to 350°F.
2. In small skillet, melt ¼ cup butter. Sauté garlic, mushrooms and shallots until limp.
3. In small saucepan, melt remaining ½ cup butter. Add flour, salt, thyme, pepper and monosodium glutamate. Stir until smooth. Gradually add milk and cook until mixture is thickened, stirring constantly. Stir in cheeses, sour cream and wine. Stir until melted.
4. In large bowl, combine cooked macaroni, cooked shrimp, garlic mixture and cheese sauce. Blend lightly. Pour into large buttered casserole. Top with crumbs.
5. Bake 45 minutes, or until bubbly and top is nicely browned.

Meats

Beef Pot Roast

6 servings
It is well to keep in mind that pot roasts, because of the simmering process, take longer to cook at high altitudes.

Flour
    4 pounds beef: chuck,
       shoulder, rump *or* brisket
    2 tablespoons cooking oil
    1 or 2 onions, sliced

2 bay leaves
1½ cups boiling water *or*
    beef stock
1 teaspoon salt
¼ teaspoon seasoned pepper

1. Sprinkle flour over meat, or dredge meat in flour.
2. In heavy skillet or Dutch oven with cover, brown meat in hot cooking oil over high heat, never allowing it to scorch. Add onions, bay leaves, boiling water or stock, salt and pepper. Cover.
3. Bake at 325°F. for 2 to 3 hours, *or* simmer on top of stove over low heat, until tender. Remove bay leaves.

Pot Roast with Beer: Substitute beer (room temperature) for boiling water or stock, or pour beer over unbrowned roast, add onion, bay leaves, salt and pepper. Cover and cook as directed.

Pot Roast with Sour Cream and Wine: Substitute ½ cup water and 1 cup dry red or white wine for boiling water or stock. Stir ⅔ cup warm dairy sour cream into gravy when meat is done. Reheat, but do not boil.

Pressure-Cooker Pot Roast: In Step 2, brown meat in oil in pressure cooker. Place rack under meat. Add onions, bay leaves, boiling water or stock, salt and pepper. Cook 1 hour at 15 pounds pressure at 5,000 feet, letting pressure drop of its own accord, or cook 1 hour at 15 pounds pressure and cool cooker quickly in cold water. (See page 13, "Pressure Cooker," for additional information, altitude and time adjustments.) Add vegetables. Re-cover. Cook 8 minutes at 15 pounds pressure. Cool cooker quickly in cold water.

Boiled Beef with Horseradish

6 to 8 servings

4 **pounds lean beef: brisket,** **bottom round** *or* **plate**	1 **onion, quartered**
6 **cups boiling water or** **more as needed**	1 **carrot, sliced into chunks**
	1 **rib celery, sliced**

Sauce:

3 **tablespoons butter**	**Salt**
4 **tablespoons all-purpose** **flour**	**Pepper**
½ **cup scalded milk**	1 **tablespoon chopped** **parsley**
3 **tablespoons prepared** **horseradish**	1 **teaspoon lemon juice**

1. Place meat in large, heavy cooking pan with cover. Add boiling water to cover. Add onion, carrot and celery. Bring to boil, skim, and cover. Reduce heat. Simmer 3 hours, or until meat is tender. Remove meat to heated platter. Keep hot. Reserve broth.
2. In small saucepan, make sauce: Melt butter and blend in flour, stirring until smooth. Add milk, 1 cup reserved meat broth, horseradish, and salt and pepper to taste. Cook over medium heat, stirring constantly, until thickened. Add parsley and lemon juice.
3. Slice meat into thin slices across the grain and serve in a deep platter, covered with hot sauce.

Sirloin Tips Emile

6 servings

2 pounds sirloin tips, cut into 1-inch cubes
¼ cup all-purpose flour
4 tablespoons butter
1½ cups boiling water
½ cup chopped onion
6 tablespoons chopped black walnuts

1 tablespoon sherry
6 teaspoons dry mustard
¾ teaspoon powdered cardamom
3 tablespoons claret *or* other red wine

1. Dredge meat in flour.
2. In large heavy skillet or Dutch oven with cover, brown floured meat in 2 tablespoons butter over medium heat. Add boiling water and chopped onion. Cover. Bring to boil. Reduce heat. Simmer 45 minutes to 1 hour, or until tender. Place meat on heated platter and pour juices from pan; reserve ½ cup.

3. Make sauce: Melt remaining 2 tablespoons butter in same cooking pan. Add walnuts and sherry. Bring to boil. Add mustard and cardamom, stirring well. Add reserved ½ cup meat juices. Bring to boil. Cook 3 to 4 minutes, covered. Remove cover and simmer to reduce and thicken liquid. Add red wine, stir quickly and pour over meat.

Sauerbraten

6 to 8 servings
The moistening agents in marinade and sour cream take away unwelcome dryness.

¾ cup beer, ale *or* dry wine
1½ cups wine *or* cider vinegar
¾ cup water
3 medium onions, sliced
2 tablespoons mixed pickling spices
3 bay leaves

4 pounds beef: boneless rump, chuck *or* round
2 tablespoons all-purpose flour
1½ teaspoons salt
⅛ teaspoon pepper
2 tablespoons cooking oil
⅓ cup gingersnap crumbs
½ cup dairy sour cream

1. In deep bowl or crock, combine beer, ale or wine with vinegar, water, onions, pickling spices and bay leaves. Place meat in marinade. Allow to marinate in refrigerator 2 to 4 days, turning occasionally.
2. Remove meat from marinade and pat dry. Reserve marinade.
3. Blend flour, salt and pepper together. Dredge meat in seasoned flour.

4. Heat cooking oil in large heavy skillet or Dutch oven with cover. Brown meat over medium-high heat, turning to brown all sides, about 15 to 20 minutes. Add ¾ cup reserved marinade. Cover. Reduce heat. Simmer over low heat for 3½ to 4 hours, or until meat is very tender. Add small amount of marinade, if necessary to prevent cooking dry. Remove meat to heated deep platter.
5. Make gravy: Drain drippings from skillet or Dutch oven. Measure and return ⅓ cup to skillet. Add gingersnap crumbs. Stir in 2 cups strained marinade. Cook over medium heat, stirring constantly, until thickened. Blend in sour cream. Heat, but do *not* boil.
6. Slice meat and pour sauce over it before serving.

Pressure-Cooker Sauerbraten: In Step 4, brown meat in pressure cooker. Place rack under meat. Add marinade and ½ cup water. Cover and cook at 15 pounds pressure for 1 hour at 5,000 feet, letting pressure drop of its own accord. (See Pressure Cooker, page 13, for additional information, altitude and time adjustments.) Prepare gravy as directed above.

Danish Meat Balls with Mashed Potatoes

6 servings

1½ pounds lean ground beef	¼ teaspoon pepper
1½ pounds lean ground pork	Flour
1½ cups chopped onion	Cooking oil
2 eggs, beaten	2 cups consommé
¾ teaspoon ground nutmeg	1 bay leaf
1½ teaspoons salt	Mashed potatoes

1. In mixing bowl, combine ground meats with onion, eggs, nutmeg, salt and pepper.
2. Shape into 1½-inch balls. Roll in flour.
3. In skillet or Dutch oven with cover, brown meat balls in hot cooking oil. Pour off excess oil. Cover with consommé. Add bay leaf. Cover.
4. Cook over low heat for 30 minutes.
5. Remove meat balls to heated platter. Thicken liquid with 1½ tablespoons flour, stirring constantly. Return meat balls to gravy.
6. Serve with mashed potatoes.

Meat Loaf with Herbs

8 servings

1½ pounds lean ground round steak
¼ pound pork sausage
1 can (10½ ounces) cream of mushroom soup
¾ cup bread crumbs
1 teaspoon dried tarragon
1 teaspoon dried sweet basil
1 teaspoon chopped chives
1 teaspoon chopped parsley
¼ cup black or green pitted chopped olives
⅛ teaspoon paprika
1 clove garlic, crushed, if desired
Mushroom Sauce, page 156

1. Preheat oven to 350°F. Lightly grease baking dish or loaf pan.
2. Mix all ingredients lightly but well. Shape into loaf and place in baking dish, or gently press into prepared loaf pan.
3. Bake for 1 hour, or until done through and well browned. Serve with Mushroom Sauce.

Beef Stroganoff
6 servings

2 pounds well-trimmed beef
  tenderloin, sliced ¼-inch
  thick and cut into
  1-by-2-inch strips
1½ tablespoons butter
1 tablespoon minced onion
1 pound fresh mushrooms,
  wiped clean (or washed

quickly and dried), and
  sliced
¾ teaspoon salt
½ teaspoon paprika
⅛ teaspoon ground nutmeg
½ teaspoon sweet basil,
  if desired
1 cup warm dairy sour
  cream

1. In heavy skillet, quickly sauté tenderloin strips in butter until evenly browned.
2. Add onion. Cook 5 minutes, turning beef to brown it. Remove beef to heated dish and keep warm.
3. Sauté mushrooms in same pan, adding butter if necessary. Add beef strips, salt, paprika, nutmeg and basil. Stir.
4. Add sour cream. Heat, but do *not* boil. Serve immediately.

Chinese Ginger Beef
6 servings

¼ cup Japanese soy sauce
  (shoyu)
2 ounces brandy *or*
  cognac
2 cloves garlic, chopped
¼ cup cornstarch
3 to 4 pounds beef
  tenderloin, cut in ¾-inch
  cubes or chunks
Cooking oil
1 tablespoon salt

1 ounce fresh ginger root,
  thinly sliced
1½ cups beef stock *or* water
½ cup water chestnuts,
  sliced
½ cup bamboo shoots, sliced
1 tablespoon monosodium
  glutamate
4 green onions, cut in
  1-inch pieces
Boiled rice

1. Make marinade: Combine soy or shoyu sauce, brandy or cognac, garlic and cornstarch. Pour over beef and marinate ½ hour or more at room temperature.
2. In large skillet, heat enough cooking oil to cover bottom of pan. Add salt. Put ginger in hot oil. Sauté until ginger begins to brown and dry up. Add beef and marinade. Sauté until lightly browned. Add beef stock or water, water chestnuts and bamboo shoots. Cover. Cook to desired doneness. If rare meat is preferred, the beef will be done as soon as the gravy boils 1 minute. If well done is preferred, add more water, stirring frequently to prevent burning. Add monosodium glutamate. Remove from heat.
3. Add green onions. Stir. Serve with boiled rice.

East Indian Beef Curry

6 servings

1 medium onion, finely chopped
2 tablespoons butter
2 tablespoons curry powder
2 cups boiling water
1½ to 2 pounds beef round steak, cut in ½-inch cubes
1½ cups canned tomatoes
1 medium potato, peeled and diced
½ teaspoon salt
1 can (4 ounces) mushrooms, drained
1 can (6 ounces) evaporated milk
2 tablespoons all-purpose flour
Juice of ½ lemon
Boiled rice

1. In large skillet or heavy saucepan, sauté onion in melted butter until limp. Add curry powder. Stir to blend. Add

boiling water, cubed round steak, tomatoes, potato and salt. Cover. Cook over medium-low heat 3½ hours.

2. Just before serving, add mushrooms and evaporated milk. Stir in flour, which has been blended to a paste with a little water; cook until thickened. Turn off heat. When sauce stops boiling, stir in lemon juice.

3. Serve over boiled rice.

Kal Dolmar

(Ground beef in cabbage leaves)   6 servings

10 to 12 large cabbage
  leaves
Boiling water
 1 pound ground beef
⅔ cup cooked rice
 1 egg, beaten
 1 teaspoon salt
½ teaspoon dried thyme
⅛ teaspoon pepper

3 tablespoons chopped
  onion
1 tablespoon chopped
  parsley
½ clove garlic, crushed,
  if desired
Butter or cooking oil
¾ cup boiling meat stock *or*
  tomato juice

1. Preheat oven to 375°F. Lightly grease large baking dish.
2. Place cabbage leaves in boiling water for 5 minutes to soften. Drain. Gently pat dry.
3. Combine remaining ingredients except butter or oil and meat stock or tomato juice. Put a generous amount of mixture on each cabbage leaf. Fold in sides, roll up, and fasten with toothpick.
4. Place closely together in baking dish. Dot rolls with butter. Pour meat stock or tomato juice over rolls.
5. Bake at 375°F. for 1 hour or until very tender, adding more stock or tomato juice if necessary to prevent sticking.

Bavarian Beef Rolls

4 servings

2 pounds round steak,
  sliced ¼-inch thick
Salt
Pepper
Prepared mustard
½ pound sliced bacon
2 dill pickles, cut into
  julienne strips

1 large onion, finely
  chopped
Flour
2 tablespoons tomato paste
2 cups beef stock, consommé
  or water
Noodles, mashed potatoes *or*
  rice

1. Preheat oven to 450°F. Lightly grease flat baking dish.
2. Cut round steak into 10 by 5-inch pieces. Sprinkle round-steak pieces with salt and pepper. Spread each piece with mustard. Place half a slice of bacon, a strip of pickle and a heaping teaspoonful of chopped onion on each piece of meat. Roll up. Fasten with toothpick.
3. Place beef rolls in baking dish. Bake in preheated oven until browned. Remove from oven. Dust with flour. Spread with tomato paste. Brown in oven again.
4. Add beef stock, consommé or water. Reduce temperature to 350°F. Bake 2 hours more, or until tender. Serve with noodles, mashed potatoes or rice.

Southwestern Frankfurters

4 to 6 servings
Use the pressure cooker to achieve this piquant flavor. These versatile frankfurters are equally good accompanying cocktails, or at children's birthday parties.

¼ cup catsup
¼ cup water
Dash liquid hot pepper sauce

Dash chili powder
1 package (1 pound)
frankfurters, thinly sliced

Place all ingredients together in pressure cooker. Cook for 1 minute at 15 pounds pressure at 5,000 feet. Cool cooker quickly in cold water. Serve on toothpicks as hors d'oeuvre, on frankfurter buns, or as a meat course.

Leg of Lamb Exotique

6 to 8 servings
An unusual flavor is imparted to lamb by the buttermilk and spice marinade.

Leg of lamb (about 5 pounds)
½ cup tarragon vinegar
 8 cups buttermilk
 2 cloves garlic, minced
 2 large onions, thinly sliced
 1 large carrot, sliced
10 whole peppercorns, crushed
12 whole cloves
 2 bay leaves
 3 juniper berries, crushed, if desired
 4 large sprigs celery leaves
½ cup finely chopped parsley

¼ teaspoon ground allspice
¼ teaspoon ground mace
¼ teaspoon marjoram
 1 teaspoon salt
½ teaspoon freshly ground black pepper
¾ cup dry white wine
¼ cup bacon drippings
½ cup currant *or* pineapple-orange jelly
 1 teaspoon grated lemon rind
Flour
Buttered noodles

1. Wipe lamb with damp cloth. Place in crock or other vessel large enough to accommodate all ingredients. Rub well with tarragon vinegar.

2. Cover with buttermilk. Add garlic, onions, carrot, pepper-corns, 5 cloves, bay leaves, juniper berries (if desired), celery leaves, parsley, allspice, mace and marjoram. Mari-nate 4 days in refrigerator, turning twice daily and being sure to keep meat covered with marinade.

3. When ready to roast, preheat oven to 450°F. Remove lamb. Strain and reserve marinade. Wipe meat dry and rub with salt and pepper. Place in roasting pan. Stud with remaining 7 cloves. Pour wine and bacon drippings over roast.

4. Roast at 450°F. for 25 minutes, then *reduce* temperature to 325°F. Continue to bake according to timetable for roasting lamb (page 22), or to desired doneness. Baste frequently with strained marinade and pan drippings.

5. Remove roast to warm platter. Skim fat from drippings and bring to boil. Stir in jelly and lemon rind. Thicken gravy to taste with a little flour mixed to a paste with water, boiling a few moments until thoroughly cooked. Serve with hot buttered noodles.

Hawaiian Barbecued Lamb Steaks or Chops

6 servings

¼ cup lemon *or* lime juice
¼ cup prepared mustard
¼ cup soy sauce
½ teaspoon ground ginger

1 teaspoon wine vinegar
Dash garlic powder, if desired
6 lamb chops (shoulder *or* loin), 1 inch thick

1. In small bowl, make marinade of all ingredients except meat. Pour over lamb in a china, enamel, or stainless-steel bowl.

2. Allow to marinate in refrigerator 4 hours, or preferably overnight, turning occasionally.
3. Drain meat well and cook over glowing charcoal 10 to 15 minutes each side, or until done as desired; or place on rack in shallow pan in oven preheated to 350°F. Bake in oven for 35 to 45 minutes, turning and basting frequently with marinade. Length of cooking time will depend on desired doneness.

Armenian Lamb Casserole

4 servings

1 green pepper, cut into strips
1 medium onion, chopped
⅓ cup olive oil
2 pounds lean boned lamb shoulder, cut in 1-inch cubes
Flour
1 can (10¾ ounces) condensed tomato soup
½ teaspoon salt
½ teaspoon garlic salt
⅛ teaspoon pepper
¼ teaspoon ground oregano
¼ teaspoon dried sweet basil
¾ cup Burgundy wine
1 eggplant (about 2 pounds)
Grated Parmesan cheese

1. Preheat oven to 375°F. Butter 3-quart flat baking dish.
2. In skillet over medium heat, sauté green pepper and onion in olive oil until limp.
3. Dredge lamb cubes in flour. Add to vegetables. Sauté lamb until browned.
4. Meanwhile, in small saucepan, combine soup, salt, garlic salt, pepper, oregano and basil. Bring to boil. Remove from heat. Add wine.

5. Peel eggplant. Cut into slices ¾ inch thick. Arrange in baking dish. Cover with sautéed meat and vegetables. Pour tomato soup mixture over eggplant. Sprinkle with grated Parmesan cheese.
6. Bake for 1 hour.

Black Forest Lamb Shanks
(*Gebäckener Lamm Schenkel*)   4 servings

4 lamb shanks	Prepared mustard
Salt	Flour
Pepper	3 cups water *or* beef stock
Garlic salt	Paprika
Onion salt	Prepared horseradish
Monosodium glutamate	

1. Preheat oven to 500°F.
2. Remove all excess fat and outer membranes from shanks. Place shanks in heavy roasting pan with cover. Sprinkle generously with salt, pepper, garlic salt, onion salt and monosodium glutamate. Coat each shank generously with mustard, turning to cover all sides.
3. Quickly brown in oven, turning to brown all sides. *Reduce* temperature to 350°F. Bake 15 minutes. Remove from oven. Set shanks aside.
4. Make gravy: Stir a little flour into pan juices. Add water or beef stock, stirring to blend. Correct seasoning. Sprinkle with paprika to taste and stir in enough horseradish to give a definite flavor.
5. Replace shanks in gravy. Cover. Cook 1 hour longer, or until meat begins to fall from bone.
6. Skim any excess fat from gravy.

Baked Sweet and Sour Lamb Chops

4 servings

4 lamb shoulder chops *or* 8 rib chops, 1 inch thick	1 teaspoon salt
¼ cup vinegar	⅛ teaspoon pepper
¼ cup firmly packed brown sugar	¼ teaspoon ground ginger
	1 medium orange, sliced
	1 medium lemon, sliced

1. Preheat oven to 325°F. Butter 1½-quart casserole with cover.
2. In heavy skillet over high heat, pan-broil chops, turning to brown both sides. Place in casserole.
3. Combine vinegar, sugar, salt, pepper and ginger. Pour over meat. Top with orange and lemon slices. Cover.
4. Bake at 325°F. for 30 minutes, or until meat is tender.
5. Serve with rice, noodles or potatoes, using the casserole juices as sauce.

Ham, Noodle and Green-Pepper Casserole

6 servings

3 cups cooked noodles, rice *or* macaroni	½ cup finely chopped celery
1 cup cooked diced or ground ham	1½ cups milk *or* tomato juice
¾ cup grated sharp Cheddar cheese	2 eggs
½ cup finely chopped green pepper	¼ teaspoon salt
	¼ teaspoon paprika *or* pepper
	Bread crumbs
	Butter

1. Preheat oven to 350°F. Grease a 2½-quart casserole.
2. Combine cooked noodles, rice or macaroni with ham, cheese, green pepper and celery.
3. In separate bowl, beat together milk, eggs, salt and paprika or pepper. Pour over noodle mixture. Spoon into prepared casserole. Sprinkle with bread crumbs. Dot with butter.
4. Bake for 40 minutes, or until golden brown and bubbly.

Ham Loaf

6 to 8 servings
A good dinner dish, this is also a superb sandwich filling.

1½ pounds lean ham ground	⅛ teaspoon pepper
1½ pounds lean pork	⅔ cup firmly packed brown
2 eggs, beaten	sugar
⅔ cup milk	2 tablespoons prepared
⅔ cup cracker crumbs	mustard
2 teaspoons grated onion	¼ teaspoon ground cloves
½ teaspoon salt	2 tablespoons cider vinegar

1. Preheat oven to 350°F. Have ready a 9 x 5 x 3-inch loaf pan.
2. In mixing bowl combine ham, pork, eggs, milk, cracker crumbs, onion, salt and pepper. Mix thoroughly.
3. Mix together brown sugar, mustard, cloves and vinegar. Either blend this mixture into the meat mixture, or spread it over the top of meat after it has been pressed into the loaf pan.
4. Bake for 1½ hours.
5. Serve hot or cold.

Pork Roast with Wine in Foil

6 servings

5-pound pork loin roast *or* 4 to 5-pound shoulder of pork
Large sheet of heavy-duty aluminum foil

1 envelope dehydrated onion soup mix
1 cup dry red wine

1. Preheat oven to 275°F.
2. Place roast in center of aluminum foil. Sprinkle meat evenly with soup mix. Place on large flat baking pan or cookie sheet.
3. Cup foil up around roast and pour wine over meat. Seal foil securely by folding.
4. Roast at 275°F. for about 5 hours, or until tender. Meat juices may be used as sauce over sliced meat, if desired.

Pork Chops à la Flamande with Broiled Apricots

6 servings

This is equally good made with ham slices. Shorten baking time if precooked ham is used.

12 rib pork chops, about ½ to ¾ inch thick
Salt
3 to 4 tablespoons cooking oil
4 cups apple cider

4½ tablespoons sugar
2 tablespoons cornstarch
6 tablespoons apple brandy (applejack)
Broiled Apricots, page 211
Watercress

1. Preheat oven to 350°F. Have ready shallow baking dish with cover.
2. Sprinkle chops generously with salt.
3. Heat oil in heavy skillet. Quickly brown the chops, slitting edges if they curl. Place chops in baking dish.
4. In saucepan, heat cider to boiling.
5. Combine sugar and cornstarch. Add to hot cider. Reduce temperature and simmer 3 to 5 minutes, stirring constantly, until sauce is clarified and thickened. (Add more cornstarch, if necessary.) Remove from heat. Add brandy and ⅛ teaspoon salt. Pour over chops. Cover.
6. Bake for 1½ hours, or until tender. Remove cover and bake 5 to 10 minutes longer if additional browning is desired.
7. Arrange chops on warm platter. Pour sauce over them. Garnish with Broiled Apricots and watercress.

Pork Teriyaki

6 servings

6 center-cut pork chops,   Teriyaki Sauce or Marinade,
  1¼ inches thick, *or*   page 163
12 slices pork tenderloin,
  1¼ inches thick

1. Place pork in 14 x 10 x 2-inch baking pan or dish. Pour Teriyaki Sauce or Marinade over meat. Turn to cover each side.
2. Marinate 4 hours, or overnight, in refrigerator. Turn occasionally.
3. Broil in same pan on lowest rack until done, turning once. Baste with marinade during broiling.

Tropical Pork

6 servings

6 lean pork chops, steaks *or*
tenderloin slices
1 teaspoon ground ginger
½ teaspoon dry mustard
1 teaspoon salt

1 tablespoon brown sugar
2 tablespoons soy sauce
2 unpeeled oranges, washed
and cut in ¼-inch slices
Powdered sugar

1. Trim excess fat from pork. Place fat in large skillet with cover and render over low heat.
2. Combine ginger, mustard, salt, sugar and soy sauce. Rub into both sides of meat.
3. Remove rendered fat. Increase heat. Brown meat on both sides in hot fat. Reduce heat, cover, and cook 35 to 40 minutes, turning once or twice, until done. Remove meat to warmed serving dish.
4. Dredge orange slices in powdered sugar. Brown in pan drippings. Arrange as garnish for meat. Spoon any remaining pan juice over meat.

Veal à la Crème

4 servings

1 pound veal, thinly sliced
or pounded and cut into
2-inch strips
4 shallots, chopped
6 large fresh mushrooms,
sliced *or*
1 can (4 ounces) sliced
mushrooms, drained
3 tablespoons butter

½ cup dry white wine
½ cup cream
½ teaspoon paprika
2 tablespoons canned
brown gravy *or*
1 teaspoon Kitchen
Bouquet
Juice of ½ lemon

1. In skillet, sauté veal, shallots and mushrooms in butter over medium heat until lightly browned. Add wine. Bring to boil. Cook 2 minutes.
2. Add cream, paprika and brown gravy or Kitchen Bouquet. Simmer 4 minutes more. Add lemon juice.
3. Serve with rice or noodles.

French Veal Stew

6 servings
This improves in flavor if refrigerated overnight and rewarmed over very low heat.

2 pounds boned veal
    shoulder, cut in ¾-inch
    cubes
Flour
  1 teaspoon salt
¼ teaspoon pepper
  2 to 3 tablespoons olive *or*
    other cooking oil
  1 large onion, studded with
    4 whole cloves
  1 quart boiling water
  3 carrots, cut in 1-inch
    pieces

  1 bay leaf
⅛ teaspoon dried thyme
  2 sprigs parsley
½ cup diced celery
  2 cloves garlic, crushed
12 small white, cooked or
    canned onions
  1 cup small canned
    mushrooms
  3 egg yolks, beaten
  2 tablespoons lemon juice
  1 tablespoon cream

1. Dust veal cubes with flour mixed with salt and pepper.
2. In Dutch oven or large heavy cooking pot with cover, quickly brown meat in oil. Add onion, boiling water, carrots, bay leaf, thyme, parsley, celery and garlic. Cover. Simmer for 1 hour.

3. Remove onion and bay leaf. Add small onions and mushrooms.
4. Combine egg yolks, lemon juice and cream. Add a little hot broth to egg mixture. Blend, and add to stew. Heat through, stirring constantly, but do not boil.

Hungarian Veal Birds

4 servings

1½ pounds veal steak,
    ½ inch thick, cut into
    8 serving pieces
 1 teaspoon salt
¼ teaspoon pepper
¼ teaspoon paprika
¼ teaspoon thyme
 1 cup soft bread crumbs
 1 tablespoon chopped
    parsley
 1 tablespoon chopped
    onion

1 tablespoon chopped
    mushrooms
½ teaspoon poultry
    seasoning
1 tablespoon chopped
    sour pickles
1 egg, beaten
¼ cup all-purpose flour
¼ cup butter *or* shortening
½ cup boiling water *or*
    stock

1. Preheat oven to 350°F. Have 2-quart casserole ready.
2. Season meat with salt, pepper, paprika and thyme.
3. Make stuffing: Combine bread crumbs, parsley, onion, mushrooms, poultry seasoning, pickle and egg. Spread stuffing over slices of seasoned meat. Roll up and secure each roll with small skewer or wooden pick, or tie closed with string. Roll in flour.
4. Melt butter or shortening in skillet. Quickly brown veal birds.

5. Place in casserole. Add boiling water or stock. Cover. Bake for 45 minutes to 1 hour, turning once, or until tender.
6. If gravy is desired, substitute cream or sour cream for water in Step 5.

Veal Scallopine with Marsala

4 to 6 servings

2 pounds veal steak,
 ½ inch thick, cut into
 2-inch strips
¼ cup all-purpose flour
1 teaspoon salt
¼ teaspoon freshly ground
 black pepper
⅛ teaspoon ground oregano
⅓ cup melted butter

⅓ cup Marsala wine
1¼ cups water
2 canned pimientos,
 drained and chopped
1 teaspoon dried parsley
 flakes
Dash dried thyme
Dash dried marjoram
Lemon wedges

1. Pound veal strips until thin.
2. Mix flour, salt, pepper and oregano. Dredge pounded meat in flour mixture, using all of flour mixture.
3. In skillet, melt butter and quickly brown floured meat. Reduce heat, cover, and simmer 15 minutes, or until veal is tender. Place veal on heated platter; keep warm.
4. Make sauce: Pour wine and water into skillet. Heat, stirring constantly, for about 5 minutes over low heat. Add pimientos, parsley, thyme and marjoram. Simmer until sauce is hot. Pour over hot meat. Garnish with lemon wedges.

Chicken Livers and Mushrooms in Madeira

6 servings

1 pound fresh chicken
   livers *or*
   2 packages (8 ounces each)
   frozen chicken livers,
   thawed
Salt
Pepper

¼ cup all-purpose flour
¼ cup butter
1 tablespoon finely chopped
   chives
1 cup sliced mushrooms
1 cup Madeira wine
1 cup beef stock

1. Salt and pepper livers. Dredge lightly in flour.
2. In skillet, melt butter. Sauté livers for about 5 minutes, turning once. Add chives and mushrooms. Cook 5 minutes more. Add Madeira wine and beef stock. Allow to simmer until slightly thickened.
3. Serve over rice or buttered toast.

Veal Sweetbreads Chablis

4 servings

2 pairs veal sweetbreads
   (about 2 pounds)
2 tablespoons mixed
   pickling spice
½ lemon, thinly sliced
Water
½ cup all-purpose flour
½ cup butter

1 cup fresh mushrooms,
   thinly sliced
½ clove garlic, thinly sliced
⅓ cup Chablis wine
1 cup chopped fresh
   tomatoes
1 shallot, finely chopped
Boiled rice

1. In medium-size saucepan, combine sweetbreads, pickling spice, lemon slices and enough water to cover. Simmer about 30 minutes.

2. Remove sweetbreads. Wash in cold water, and remove veins. Cut in half.
3. Dredge cooked sweetbreads in flour, or shake in flour in paper bag.
4. In skillet large enough to accommodate all ingredients, melt butter. Sauté floured sweetbreads for 15 minutes, covered, so as not to lose moisture. Add mushrooms, garlic, wine, tomatoes and chopped shallot. Re-cover pan, and simmer 15 minutes longer. Serve over boiled rice.

Boiled Fresh, Corned or Smoked Beef Tongue

Allow 1 pound cooked tongue for 4 servings

1 beef tongue	1 tablespoon vinegar
(2 to 5 pounds)	Boiling water
6 peppercorns	Mustard Sauce, page 161,
1 tablespoon brown sugar	or Green Pepper Sauce,
4 whole cloves	page 159
½ teaspoon powdered thyme	

1. Scrub tongue under cold running water. Place in Dutch oven or large, deep kettle with tight-fitting cover. Add peppercorns, sugar, cloves, powdered thyme, vinegar and enough boiling water to cover. Cover.
2. Bring to boil. Reduce heat. Simmer 2 to 4½ hours, or until a fork will penetrate readily to center of meat, depending on freshness and size of tongue. Allow tongue to remain in cooking water until cool enough to handle.
3. Peel off outer skin, cut out membraneous portions, and press into shape for serving.
4. Slice and serve hot, or cool and serve with Mustard Sauce, or Green Pepper Sauce.

Poultry

Chicken à la Kiev

6 servings

Breasts of 3 large chickens
Garlic powder
Crushed dried tarragon,
 to taste
¼ pound hard butter
1 cup all-purpose flour

4 eggs, beaten with ½ cup
 milk
3 cups sifted bread crumbs
Hot cooking oil
Mushroom Sauce, page 156

1. Bone chicken breasts, remove skin, and divide each lengthwise into 2 pieces. Flatten slightly with cleaver. Season
   lightly with garlic powder and tarragon to taste.
2. Cut butter into 6 pieces and place one on each half breast,
   rolling chicken around butter securely and fastening with
   toothpick.
3. Dip stuffed, rolled breasts in flour, then into egg-milk
   wash.
4. Roll in sifted bread crumbs.
5. Fry quickly in hot cooking oil at least 1-inch deep, turning to brown all sides evenly.
6. Remove toothpicks, arrange on hot platter, and serve immediately with Mushroom Sauce.

Baked Chicken with Tomato Slices

6 servings

4 each breasts, legs and
thighs of broiler-fryer
chickens
12 slices tomato
Salt
Pepper

Paprika
1 cup grated sharp Cheddar
cheese
2 cans (10½ ounces each)
cream of chicken soup
2 to 3 tablespoons cream

1. Preheat oven to 350°F. Butter large shallow baking dish.
2. Place chicken pieces in baking dish. Cover each piece of chicken with a slice of tomato. Add salt and pepper to taste. Sprinkle with paprika. Cover with grated cheese.
3. Thin soup with cream to desired consistency. Pour over cheese.
4. Bake for 1 hour, or until chicken is tender.

Custard Chicken

10 servings

Butter
Parsley sprigs
1 large chicken, cooked,
boned and diced
1½ cups milk

4 eggs, slightly beaten
½ teaspoon salt
Cayenne pepper, to taste
1 tablespoon cornstarch
White Sauce, page 155

1. Preheat oven to 350°F. Butter 10 individual molds or custard cups.
2. Place a parsley sprig in bottom of each mold. Arrange chicken in molds.

3. Mix together milk, eggs, salt, cayenne pepper, and cornstarch. Pour over chicken.
4. Place in shallow pan on oven rack. Pour boiling water into pan to depth of 1 inch.
5. Bake for about 30 minutes, or until custard sets. Serve with White Sauce.

Chicken in Wine with Barley

4 servings

1 broiler-fryer chicken (about 3 pounds), quartered	¼ teaspoon dried rosemary
	Paprika
	½ cup barley
1 can (10½ ounces) cream of mushroom soup	1 cup chicken broth
	½ teaspoon salt
1 cup dairy sour cream	1 lemon, quartered
½ cup sherry	

1. Preheat oven to 350°F. Butter covered 1½-quart baking dish.
2. Wash and pat chicken quarters dry. Place in prepared baking dish.
3. Mix together mushroom soup, sour cream and sherry. Pour over chicken. Sprinkle with rosemary and paprika. Cover.
4. Bake for 1 hour or longer, or until tender.
5. Meanwhile, wash barley well. Place in saucepan with chicken broth and salt. Bring to boil. Cover, reduce heat, and steam 40 minutes, or until tender.
6. Serve chicken and sauce over steamed barley. Serve with lemon quarters, to be squeezed over each serving.

Chicken Royale

4 servings

2 broiler-fryer chickens
(2½ to 3 pounds each), *or*
4 whole chicken breasts,
cut in half
Salt
Pepper

¼ cup butter
Juice of ½ lemon
2 shallots, finely chopped
½ cup dry white wine
½ cup coarsely chopped
walnuts

1. Sprinkle chicken pieces with salt and pepper.
2. In large skillet, melt butter. Add lemon juice. When butter bubbles, brown chicken pieces quickly on both sides, about 10 to 12 minutes. Add shallots. Cook 2 to 3 minutes. Add wine. Cover pan tightly. Continue cooking over low heat until chicken is tender.
3. Roast walnuts in moderate oven for about 10 minutes. Sprinkle with salt.
4. Five minutes before the chicken is done, add walnuts.

Chicken Smothered in Vermouth

4 servings

1 broiler-fryer (about
3 pounds), quartered
½ cup all-purpose flour
3 tablespoons butter *or*
cooking oil
2 cups vermouth *or* dry
sauterne

4 tomatoes, peeled and
quartered
2 stalks celery, sliced
4 very large mushrooms,
washed and dried

1. Preheat oven to 350°F. Have casserole with cover ready.
2. Wash and pat chicken quarters dry. Dredge with flour.
3. In skillet, brown chicken in butter or cooking oil over medium-high heat. Place in casserole. Pour vermouth or sauterne over browned chicken. Add tomatoes, celery and mushrooms. Cover.
4. Bake at 350°F. for 1½ to 2 hours, or until tender.

Rock Cornish Hens Français

4 servings

4 Rock Cornish game
  hens *or*
  4 whole medium-size
  broiler-fryer chicken
  breasts
4 thin slices smoked ham
4 slices Swiss cheese,
  about 1 by 3 inches
1 cup all-purpose flour
½ teaspoon garlic salt
½ teaspoon pepper

½ teaspoon ground thyme
½ teaspoon paprika
1 egg, mixed with
  2 tablespoons milk
1½ cups cracker crumbs
½ cup cooking oil
1 cup Medium White
  Sauce, page 155
1 tablespoon sherry
1 teaspoon grated
  Parmesan cheese

1. Preheat oven to 350°F. Have ready shallow baking dish.
2. Strip breastbone from Cornish hens, leaving ½-inch neck bone for finger holder, or have broiler-fryer breasts halved, boned and flattened. Press hens or breasts as flat as possible with hands.
3. Place slice of ham and slice of cheese on top of each hen or breast. Roll breast meat around ham and cheese. Secure with toothpicks, or tie securely.

4. Mix together flour, garlic, salt, pepper, thyme and paprika. Dredge rolled breasts or hens in seasoned flour.
5. Dip in egg and milk mixture. Roll in cracker crumbs.
6. In skillet over medium heat, brown in cooking oil until golden. Drain on paper toweling. Place in baking dish.
7. Bake at 350°F. for 40 to 50 minutes.
8. Combine Medium White Sauce, dry sherry and grated Parmesan cheese. Heat through, but do not boil. Spoon sauce over baked stuffed birds or breasts.

Duck on a Spit

4 servings

1 Long Island duckling (5 pounds)	½ cup olive oil
Salt	½ cup sweet vermouth
Pepper	1 large orange, quartered
Monosodium glutamate	12 cloves

1. Wash duckling and pat dry. Have oven preheated to 360°F., or charcoal glowing in outdoor rotisserie.
2. Sprinkle cavity of duckling with salt, pepper and mono-sodium glutamate.
3. Combine olive oil and vermouth. Brush duckling with mixture.
4. Stud orange quarters with cloves and place in cavity of duckling.
5. Tie or otherwise fasten bird securely on spit. Insert meat thermometer into thick part of thigh, near body. Roast

at 360°F. for 2 hours, basting with vermouth-oil mixture, or until meat thermometer reads 195°F. If rotisserie is used, roast over glowing charcoal, basting frequently, until the same reading is reached; exact time will depend on heat of coals.

Turkey or Chicken Casserole with Wild Rice

8 servings

1½ cups uncooked wild rice
4 cups water
1½ teaspoons salt
1 pound good bulk pork
sausage
1 can (3 ounces)
mushrooms, drained
2 cans (10½ ounces each)
cream of mushroom soup

1½ teaspoons Worcestershire
sauce
Few grains cayenne pepper
8 large or 16 small slices
cooked turkey *or* chicken
Buttered Bread Crumbs,
page 75

1. Preheat oven to 375°F. Grease a 12 x 8 x 2-inch baking dish.
2. Wash wild rice well with lukewarm water. Put rice, water and salt in saucepan. Bring to boil. Cover, reduce heat and cook until done and all water is absorbed—about 30 to 45 minutes.
3. Meanwhile, cook sausage in skillet over medium heat, breaking into small granules as it browns. Drain off fat during cooking. Stir in cooked wild rice, mushrooms, soup, Worcestershire sauce and cayenne pepper. Heat through, but do not boil.
4. Spread one-half of cooked rice mixture in prepared baking

dish. Cover with turkey or chicken slices and top with remaining rice mixture.

5. Sprinkle with Buttered Bread Crumbs.
6. Bake for 40 minutes, or until golden brown and bubbly.

Turkey or Chicken Marengo

8 servings

1 turkey *or* chicken (5 pounds), cut in serving-size pieces
1 cup all-purpose flour
1 teaspoon salt
¼ teaspoon pepper
1 teaspoon dried marjoram
¼ cup olive *or* other cooking oil
1 cup chopped onion
1 clove garlic, crushed

1 can (10½ ounces) chicken consommé
8 medium tomatoes, peeled and chopped
½ pound fresh mushrooms, washed and sliced
2 tablespoons cognac
Buttered Bread Crumbs, page 75
Chopped parsley

1. Preheat oven to 375°F. Have ready a shallow baking dish with cover.
2. Wash turkey or chicken and pat dry.
3. Mix together flour, salt, pepper and marjoram. Dredge poultry pieces in seasoned flour; reserve unused flour.
4. In skillet, brown turkey or chicken pieces in hot oil. Place in baking dish. Reserve pan drippings.
5. In pan drippings, sauté onion and garlic until limp. Add remaining flour mixture. Stir until smooth. Add chicken consommé. Cook until bubbly. Stir in tomatoes and mushrooms. Bring to boil. Remove at once from heat.
6. Pour sauce over turkey or chicken. Cover.

7. Bake for 1½ hours, or until tender. Uncover, and continue baking 10 minutes longer to brown evenly. Sprinkle with cognac.
8. Sprinkle with Buttered Bread Crumbs. Place under broiler for 2 minutes, or until browned.
9. Garnish with parsley and serve with boiled rice.

Curried Turkey or Chicken and Mushrooms
6 servings

4 tablespoons butter
½ cup finely chopped onion
½ cup finely chopped green pepper
3 tablespoons all-purpose flour
2 to 3 teaspoons curry powder *or* to taste
1 teaspoon salt
Few grains cayenne pepper

2 cups chicken broth *or* 4 chicken bouillon cubes and 2 cups boiling water
3 cups diced cooked turkey *or* chicken
¾ cup sliced mushrooms
½ cup slivered almonds
Boiled rice
Sambals for Curry (page 161)

1. In large heavy saucepan with cover, melt butter. Sauté onion and green pepper in melted butter until limp. Remove from heat. Blend in flour, curry powder, salt and cayenne pepper.
2. In saucepan, heat broth or dissolve bouillon cubes in boiling water. Stir into onion mixture. Cook, stirring constantly, until sauce comes to boil and is thickened.
3. Add turkey or chicken, mushrooms and almonds. Simmer, covered, for 15 minutes, or until flavors have blended.
4. Serve over boiled rice with Sambals for Curry.

Turkey or Chicken with Cashews

4 to 6 servings

4 cups, cooked, diced
  turkey *or* chicken (canned
  poultry may be used)
2 cans (4 ounces each)
  mushroom stems, pieces
  and liquid
2 cups condensed cream of
  mushroom soup

1 cup cashews
1½ cups chopped celery
1 medium onion, finely
  chopped
1 can (3 ounces) chow-mein
  noodles

1. Preheat oven to 325°F. Butter 2-quart casserole.
2. Mix all ingredients together, reserving 1½ tablespoons noodles for top. Pour into prepared casserole.
3. Bake for 50 minutes. Sprinkle with reserved noodles. Bake 10 minutes more.

Game & Game Birds

Venison, Elk or Antelope Pot Roast

6 servings

Pot roasting is a method that combats the dryness of game.

4- to 5-pound venison, elk or antelope pot roast	2 teaspoons salt
	¼ teaspoon pepper
4 slices bacon *or* salt pork	¼ cup all-purpose flour
3 medium onions, chopped	4 cups beef stock,
1 stalk celery, chopped	consommé *or* water
1 bay leaf	1 cup cream
1 carrot, chopped	2 cups button mushrooms

1. Preheat oven to 450°F.
2. Remove all fat, cartilage and outer membranes from meat. Bard (wrap) meat with bacon or salt pork slices. Place meat in roasting pan with cover. Add onions, celery, bay leaf, carrot, salt and pepper. Cover.
3. Bake at 450°F. for 20 minutes. *Reduce* temperature to 300°F. Cook about 3 hours longer, or until tender. Remove meat to a warmed serving dish and keep hot.
4. In same pan, sprinkle vegetables and drippings with flour; stir well. Add beef stock, consommé or water. Cook over medium heat until liquid is reduced to 2 cups. Strain. Add cream. Cook until golden brown. Add mushrooms to sauce. Pour over meat.

Marinated Venison, Elk or Antelope

4 to 6 servings

Roasts of shoulder meat and other less choice cuts are successfully prepared this way, as are loins and legs. Kebab-size chunks are delicious marinated, then skewered and broiled.

2 to 4 pounds venison, elk *or* antelope meat
2 cups cider, sauterne *or* claret wine
½ cup vinegar
Juice of 2 lemons *or* limes
1 onion, sliced
1 carrot, diced
2 stalks celery, diced
1 clove garlic, mashed
4 sprigs parsley
1 bay leaf
2 peppercorns *or* ¼ teaspoon pepper
¼ teaspoon ground thyme
½ cup cooking or olive oil *or* salt pork or bacon slices
½ cup currant jelly

1. Remove all fat, cartilage and surface membrane from meat.
2. In large enamel or crockery pan or bowl, combine all ingredients except meat and oil; or salt pork or bacon; and currant jelly. Mix well. Add meat.
3. Allow to marinate in refrigerator overnight, or for as long as 3 days, turning meat frequently.
4. Preheat oven to 375°F.
5. Drain meat, reserving marinade. Place meat in roasting pan. Generously brush with cooking or olive oil, or cover with salt pork or bacon slices. Strain marinade.
6. Roast meat according to cut, following timetable for roasting beef (page 19). Baste frequently with marinade.
7. Make gravy: Press pan drippings through sieve. Mix with currant jelly and bring to boil, stirring constantly.

Pan-fried Venison Steaks or Chops

2 servings

One of the best ways to prepare the better cuts of wild game is fast pan-frying to doneness, then adding a savory sauce.

2 tablespoons butter *or* olive oil	Pepper
	Paprika
1 clove garlic, cut in half, if desired	¼ cup dry sherry
	¼ cup cream
2 venison steaks *or* chops	2 tablespoons butter
Salt	1½ tablespoons currant jelly

1. In large skillet, heat butter or olive oil, add garlic, if desired. Add meat and brown on one side. Turn and brown on other. Season with salt, pepper and paprika. Reduce heat. Cook just until well done on outside and juicy red or pink inside. Remove garlic.
2. Add sherry, cream, butter and jelly to pan. Stir until all ingredients are blended. Baste steaks or chops until well coated.
3. Serve on well-heated platter, with sauce spooned over meat.

Smothered Rabbit with Fruit Juice

4 to 6 servings

1 cup dried pitted prunes	Salt
2 cups water *or*	Pepper
1 cup water and 1 cup white wine	3 tablespoons cooking oil *or* shortening
1 rabbit (3 to 4 pounds), cut up	

1. Soak prunes for 4 to 5 hours in 1 cup water, or ½ cup water and ½ cup wine.
2. Wash rabbit pieces thoroughly. Pat dry. Sprinkle with salt and pepper.
3. In heavy cooking pan with cover, brown rabbit in hot oil or shortening. Add remaining 1 cup water, or ½ cup water and ½ cup wine. Simmer, covered, over low heat for 1½ to 2 hours.
4. About 15 minutes before end of cooking period, add prunes.

Rabbit Italienne

4 servings

2½-pound rabbit, cut into pieces
½ cup all-purpose flour
1 teaspoon salt
⅛ teaspoon pepper
⅛ teaspoon paprika
¼ cup olive oil
1 large onion, chopped
1 clove garlic, minced

2 tablespoons chopped fresh parsley
1 can (8 ounces) tomato sauce
1 cup dry red wine
1 bay leaf
⅛ teaspoon dried oregano
⅛ teaspoon dried sweet basil

1. Wash rabbit pieces; pat dry.
2. Mix flour, salt, pepper and paprika; dredge rabbit pieces.
3. In Dutch oven or heavy pan with cover, brown rabbit in olive oil; remove and set aside.
4. Sauté onion in pan drippings until limp. Add garlic and parsley, cooking just until well coated with oil. Add

tomato sauce, wine, bay leaf, oregano and basil. Simmer 20 minutes, stirring occasionally.

5. Replace rabbit in pan with sauce. Cover. Simmer over low heat for about 45 minutes to 1 hour, or until rabbit is tender; or cook in oven preheated to 325°F. for 1 to 1½ hours, or until tender.

Baked Dove Breasts

4 to 5 servings
Cream and wine give these rare morsels a royal treatment.

12 dove breasts	Salt
2 cups sherry	Pepper
6 tablespoons all-purpose flour	4 tablespoons cooking oil
	1 cup cream

1. Wash dove breasts thoroughly in cold water. Drain well. Pat dry. Place in shallow baking pan. Pour 1 cup sherry over breasts. Marinate in refrigerator for 5 hours, turning occasionally.
2. Remove breasts from sherry. Discard wine.
3. Preheat oven to 325°F.
4. Season flour with salt and pepper to taste. Dredge breasts in seasoned flour.
5. In skillet, lightly brown breasts in hot cooking oil. Remove and place in shallow baking pan.
6. Combine remaining 1 cup sherry with cream. Pour over breasts.
7. Bake for 30 to 40 minutes or until tender, basting every 10 minutes with sherry-cream mixture.

Roast Wild Duck I

Allow one-half duck per person

Wild ducks	Apple, chopped
Seasoned salt	Bacon drippings *or* shortening
Seasoned pepper	Melted butter
Celery, coarsely chopped	Madeira *or* dry sauterne
Green or dry onions, chopped	wine, if desired

1. Preheat oven to 450°F.
2. Wash ducks thoroughly in cold water. Drain well; pat dry inside and out. Remove fat gland at base of tail. Sprinkle cavity with seasoned salt and pepper. Stuff each duck with equal amounts of celery, dry or green onions (tops included) and apple. If duck is not young, soak a small piece of cheesecloth in vinegar and place in lower cavity at base of tail. Rub skin well with bacon drippings or shortening.
3. Place on rack in roasting pan with breast side up or down, as preferred.
4. For rare duck, roast 18 minutes per pound; for medium duck, roast 22 minutes per pound. If desired, baste with butter and Madeira or dry sauterne wine.
5. Let stand 10 minutes on warmed platter before carving. (The stuffing is for flavoring only, and is not to be served.)

Roast Wild Duck II: This method is for rare to medium-rare duck. Have duck at room temperature for 4 hours. If desired, stuff as directed for Roast Wild Duck I. Add small amount of water to pan. Preheat oven to 500° to 550°F. and roast for 20 to 30 minutes, depending on size of duck and degree of doneness desired. Allow duck to stand 7 to 10 minutes on warmed serving dish before carving. Serve with

½ cup melted butter mixed and heated with 3 tablespoons lemon juice.

Roast Teal I: Follow directions for preparing Roast Wild Duck I for the oven. Roast teal with breast down for 30 to 34 minutes, depending on size of bird and degree of doneness desired.

Roast Teal II: This method is for rare to medium-rare teal. Follow directions for Roast Wild Duck II. Roast for 12 to 14 minutes, depending on size of bird and degree of rareness desired.

Wild Duck Maison

4 servings

2 wild ducks
4 tablespoons butter
½ cup Marsala *or* sherry
2 tablespoons tomato paste
3 tablespoons all-purpose
flour *or*
2 tablespoons potato flour
1½ cups chicken stock *or*
consommé
1 teaspoon salt
¼ teaspoon pepper

1 bay leaf
¼ to ½ pound fresh
mushrooms, sliced
1 pimiento, diced
½ green pepper, diced,
if desired
3 tomatoes, peeled and
chopped
1 teaspoon grated orange
rind
6 orange sections

1. Wash ducks thoroughly in cold water. Drain well and pat dry. Remove fat at base of tails, cut into pieces and discard wings.
2. In large Dutch oven or heavy pan with cover, brown duck

in 2 tablespoons butter over medium heat. Add wine. Remove duck.

3. Stir tomato paste and flour into pan. Blend well. Add chicken stock and bring to boil. Replace duck pieces in stock. Season with salt, pepper, and add bay leaf. Cover and cook 1 hour and 15 minutes over low heat.

4. In skillet sauté sliced mushrooms in remaining 2 tablespoons butter over low heat. Add pimiento, green pepper, chopped tomato, orange rind, and orange sections. Cook over low heat for a few minutes.

5. Remove duck and place on warmed serving dish or platter.

6. Skim grease from juices in pan. Remove bay leaf. If not consistency of gravy, thicken with a little additional flour. Add mushroom mixture. Reheat. Spoon over duck. Garnish with border of spiced crabapples, if desired.

Roast Wild Goose I

4 to 6 servings

Sauerkraut Stuffing, page 168, may be used in place of the seasoning vegetables listed in the recipe. Although made inedible by the excess grease from the goose, it absorbs the gaminess that is objectionable to some.

1 wild goose (4 to 6 pounds)	Bacon *or* sausage drippings
Salt	2 cups chicken stock *or*
Pepper	bouillon
½ cup coarsely chopped celery	1 tablespoon all-purpose flour
⅓ cup coarsely chopped green *or* dry onions	1¾ cups currant jelly
1 cup chopped apple	2 to 3 tablespoons sherry

1. Preheat oven to 500°F.
2. Wash goose thoroughly in cold water. Drain well and pat dry inside and out. Remove fat gland at base of tail. Sprinkle cavity with salt and pepper. Stuff with equal amounts of celery, dry onions or green onions (tops included), and apple. If goose is not young, soak a small piece of cheesecloth in vinegar and place in cavity at base of tail before stuffing.
3. Rub skin well with bacon or sausage drippings.
4. Place goose on rack breast side up, or on V-shaped rack with breast side down, if preferred.
5. Roast at 500°F. for 15 minutes. *Reduce* temperature to 350°F. Roast 2½ to 3 hours more, basting frequently. If breast side is down, turn breast side up when three-fourths cooked.
6. Remove goose from oven. Let stand 10 minutes before carving.
7. In small saucepan, make gravy: Thicken chicken bouillon with a little flour, stirred to a paste with cold water. Skim excess fat from pan drippings. Add 2 tablespoons fat-free drippings. Cook over low heat until well blended. Add currant jelly and sherry; reheat, but do not boil.

Roast Wild Goose II: Have goose at room temperature for 4 hours. Stuff as directed for Roast Wild Goose I, or use Sauerkraut Stuffing, page 168. Place breast side up on rack in roasting pan. Add a little water. Bake at 500° F. for about 50 minutes.

Roast Wild Goose Pique-Nique: Because people are so accustomed to eating hot roast goose, this completely pleasing way is often overlooked. Follow directions for Roast

Goose II. After roasting, let cool, then refrigerate. Serve cold, sliced, with well-buttered bread, salt and pepper.

Stewed Partridge

Allow one-half large partridge per person

At high altitudes these birds are best sautéed, smothered or stewed. Chicken or pheasant recipes can also be used.

For each partridge:

1 bay leaf	Salt
1 clove garlic, crushed	1 slice bacon
2 peppercorns	2 cups water
3 tablespoons melted butter	

1. Dampen clean cloth with hot water. Clean bird well inside and out.
2. Place bay leaf, garlic and peppercorns in cavity. Tie legs and wings close to body. Brush generously with melted butter. Sprinkle with salt. Place bacon over breast.
3. Place partridge in Dutch oven. Add water. Cover. Bring to boil, reduce heat. Simmer over low heat for 1½ to 2 hours, or until legs will separate from body. Remove partridge to heated platter. Keep warm. Remove bay leaf and peppercorns from pan drippings. For each 1 cup liquid remaining in pan, make a paste of 1 tablespoon flour and a little water. Add to liquid. Blend well. Cook, stirring constantly, over medium-low heat until thickened. Serve with partridge.

Roast Spiced Pheasant in Sauce

6 servings

*Carry this dish covered to the table: the wonderful fruit,
herb and game perfume is too good not to be shared.*

3 young pheasants
Salt
Pepper
3 cloves garlic, peeled
3 whole cloves
3 tablespoons chopped
parsley
3 tablespoons chopped
celery

3 tablespoons chopped apple
3 thin slices lemon
6 slices bacon
1 cup Tokay wine
1 cup chicken stock
½ cup chopped onion
4 tablespoons currant jelly

1. Preheat oven to 375°F.
2. Wash pheasant thoroughly in cold water. Drain well. Pat
   dry inside and out.
3. Sprinkle cavity of each bird with salt and pepper. Stuff
   with 1 clove garlic, 1 whole clove, 1 tablespoon parsley,
   1 tablespoon chopped celery, 1 tablespoon chopped apple
   and 1 slice lemon.
4. Arrange pheasants in roasting pan. Place 2 slices bacon
   over each breast. Add wine, chicken stock and onions.
5. Roast for 1 to 1½ hours, basting frequently. Remove to
   heated serving dish.
6. Strain pan juices. Add currant jelly to juices. Heat. Serve
   with pheasants.

Sauces, Glazes, Marinades & Stuffings

Almondine Sauce

1 cup
Delicious on hot vegetables, fish, and steak.

½ cup butter
⅓ cup slivered almonds

¼ teaspoon salt
2 tablespoons lemon juice

1. In saucepan melt butter. Add almonds and brown lightly.
2. Remove from heat. Add salt and lemon juice.

Barbecue Sauce

2½ cups

2 cups canned tomatoes, chopped
⅓ cup water
2 tablespoons sugar
2 tablespoons brown sugar
¼ cup vinegar
2 tablespoons Worcestershire sauce

1½ teaspoons salt
¼ teaspoon garlic salt
1½ teaspoons chili powder
Dash cayenne pepper, and/*or* dash liquid hot pepper sauce
¾ teaspoon dry mustard

1. In saucepan, combine all ingredients. Bring to boil. Reduce heat.
2. Simmer uncovered 1 hour, or until sauce reaches desired thickness.

White Sauce

(*Béchamel Sauce*)   1 cup

For creaming vegetables, meats and fish, and as a base for other sauces. Margarine may be substituted for butter, but the flavor will not be as good. A heavy saucepan instead of a double boiler is recommended to obtain maximum gelatinization of starch at high altitudes.

	Butter	All-Purpose Flour	Milk	Salt	Pepper
Thin	1 tablespoon	1 tablespoon	1 cup	½ teaspoon	⅛ teaspoon
Medium	2 tablespoons	2 tablespoons	1 cup	½ teaspoon	⅛ teaspoon
Thick	3 tablespoons	3 tablespoons	1 cup	½ teaspoon	⅛ teaspoon

1. In small heavy saucepan, melt butter over low heat. Add flour, blending with wooden spoon until smooth. Cook for 2 minutes, stirring constantly.
2. Slowly stir in milk. Cook, stirring constantly with wire whisk or wooden spoon, until thickened, smooth and thoroughly cooked.
3. Add salt and pepper.

Anchovy Sauce: Add 3 mashed anchovy fillets to 1 cup Medium White Sauce.

Cheese Sauce (for au gratin dishes): Add 1 cup grated sharp American cheese to 1 cup Medium White Sauce. Heat, stirring constantly, until cheese is melted.

Egg Cream Sauce: Add 2 chopped hard-cooked eggs and 1 tablespoon finely chopped pickles to 1 cup Medium White Sauce.

Horseradish Sauce (Sauce Albert): Add 3 tablespoons prepared horseradish, 2 tablespoons whipping cream, 1 teaspoon granulated sugar, 1 teaspoon dry mustard and 1 tablespoon wine vinegar to 1 cup Thin White Sauce.

Cheddar Cheese Sauce: Add ¾ cup grated sharp cheddar cheese, ½ teaspoon prepared mustard, ½ teaspoon Worcestershire sauce and dash of cayenne pepper to 1 cup Medium White Sauce.

Mushroom Sauce: Add 1 cup chopped cooked mushrooms to 1 cup Thin White Sauce.

Oyster Sauce (for fish): Add 1 teaspoon Worcestershire sauce, ¼ teaspoon salt, 2 tablespoons chopped parsley and 1 cup chopped poached oysters and juice to 1 cup Medium White Sauce.

Romano Cheese Sauce: Add 1 cup grated Romano cheese and ½ teaspoon dry mustard and a dash of cayenne pepper to 1 cup Thin White Sauce.

Béarnaise Sauce

About ¾ cup
For any red meat, especially beefsteak, but equally delicious on fish or eggs.

¼ cup butter
 2 tablespoons hot water
 2 egg yolks
 1 tablespoon tarragon
   vinegar

1 teaspoon finely chopped
  shallot *or* onion
¾ teaspoon finely chopped
  parsley
⅛ teaspoon salt
Paprika

1. In top of double boiler over boiling water, melt butter with hot water. Stir in egg yolks. Beat with wire whisk or rotary beater until frothy. Stir in vinegar, shallots or onion, parsley, salt and paprika to taste.
2. Cook, stirring constantly, just until thickened and smooth, about 8 minutes. Remove double-boiler top from heat at once.
3. Serve warm.

Sauce Chablis

About 1 cup
A delicate sauce for poached flounder, sole or turbot.

½ cup Chablis wine
 2 tablespoons fresh lemon
   juice
½ bay leaf
¼ teaspoon salt
 6 peppercorns

Water
1 tablespoon butter
1 tablespoon all-purpose
  flour
2 egg yolks, beaten with
  1 tablespoon water

1. In small heavy saucepan, combine Chablis wine, lemon juice, bay leaf, salt and peppercorns. Cook 5 minutes over low heat, stirring to blend. Strain sauce, adding enough water to make 1 cup.
2. In separate saucepan, melt butter; stir in flour. Add strained liquids. Cook over medium heat, stirring constantly, until thickened. Beat a little hot sauce into beaten egg yolks, then add yolk mixture to saucepan. Cook over low heat, stirring vigorously, just until thickened—one minute or so.
3. Serve hot.

Creole Sauce

About 4 cups

2 medium onions, chopped
2 medium green peppers, chopped
½ cup butter
½ pound fresh mushrooms, cleaned and sliced
1 cup dry sauterne wine
2 large tomatoes, peeled and chopped

1 cup tomato juice
1 cup beef consommé
Cornstarch, if needed
½ clove garlic, crushed
2 sprigs parsley, chopped
Pinch of dried thyme
½ teaspoon saffron
Salt
Pepper

1. In large heavy skillet over medium heat, melt butter and sauté onion and green pepper until limp. Add mushrooms. Sauté lightly.
2. Add wine, tomatoes, tomato juice and consommé. Bring to boil. Reduce heat. Simmer for 30 minutes, or until vegetables are tender, stirring occasionally. If sauce is too

thin, thicken with a little cornstarch mixed in water. Add garlic, parsley and thyme.
3. Rub saffron between fingers until powdery. Sprinkle over sauce. Add salt and pepper to taste. Stir to blend.

Chasseur Sauce

2 cups

2 tablespoons minced
  shallots *or* onion
2 tablespoons butter
1 cup sliced mushrooms
½ cup dry white wine
1 tablespoon brandy

½ cup tomato sauce
1 cup canned brown gravy
Salt
Pepper
1 teaspoon chopped parsley

1. In small heavy saucepan, sauté shallots or onion in butter until limp. Add mushrooms and brown lightly. Stir in wine and brandy. Simmer until reduced by one half.
2. Add tomato sauce and beef gravy. Cook 5 minutes. Add salt and pepper to taste and parsley. Serve hot.

Green Pepper Sauce

About 5 cups
For beefsteaks, ground beef, pork chops, meat loaf or liver.

4 medium green peppers,
  coarsely chopped
3 tablespoons butter
4 cups brown gravy

Dash garlic powder, if desired
¼ cup Burgundy *or* dry
  sherry

1. In skillet, sauté green peppers in butter until limp.
2. Add gravy and stir over heat until smooth. Add garlic powder, if desired. Cook over medium-low heat for 5 minutes. Add wine. Remove from heat. Serve hot.

Currant Jelly Sauce

1 cup
Classic sauce for wild game birds.

  1 glass (6 ounces) currant jelly
Juice of 1 orange
¼ teaspoon dry mustard

In mixing bowl, combine all ingredients.

Curry Sauce

About 4 cups

3 medium onions, chopped
3 to 4 tablespoons butter *or* olive oil
1 teaspoon ground ginger
2 teaspoons ground cumin (*cominos*)
2 teaspoons garlic powder
1 tablespoon curry powder *or* to taste

Flour
 1 can (No. 2) tomatoes, finely chopped, and juice
1 cup dairy sour cream
1 cup buttermilk
¼ cup coconut syrup
Salt

1. In large heavy skillet over medium heat, sauté onions in butter or olive oil until limp. Blend in ginger, cumin,

garlic and curry powder. Blend completely, then blend in a little flour to make paste.
2. Add tomatoes and juice.
3. Blend in sour cream, buttermilk, and coconut syrup. Season to taste with salt. Heat through, but do not boil.

Sambals for Curry: In individual small dishes, offer any or all of these accompaniments: Chutney, raisins, snipped parsley, pineapple chunks, crisp bacon bits, chopped hard-cooked eggs, sliced bananas sprinkled with lemon and chili, shredded coconut, hot cucumber relish, onion and red pepper relish, toasted coconut chips, apple relish, chopped salted peanuts, grated orange rind, dried currants.

Mustard Sauce

About 1½ cups
For poached or broiled fish or for ham or tongue.

1 tablespoon butter	¼ teaspoon Worcestershire
2 tablespoons all-purpose	sauce
flour	1 cup half-and-half cream
½ teaspoon salt	1½ tablespoons prepared
¼ teaspoon paprika	mustard *or*
	2 teaspoons dry mustard

1. In small heavy saucepan, melt butter and add flour, stirring until smooth. Add salt, paprika and Worcestershire sauce. Add half-and-half and mustard, blending well.
2. Cook over medium-low heat, stirring constantly, until smooth and thickened, about 5 minutes or more. Serve hot.

Mint Sauce

¾ cup
Particularly delicious with roast lamb.

½ cup mint jelly
Grated rind of 1 lemon
  2 tablespoons lemon juice

Salt
½ teaspoon crushed mint
  leaves

Combine all ingredients in top of double boiler. Heat, beating to blend.

Piquant Sauce

1¼ cups
For seafood, hamburgers and frankfurters.

1 cup chili sauce *or*
  1 cup catsup
2 tablespoons prepared
  mustard

2 teaspoons sherry,
  if desired, *or*
2 teaspoons horseradish,
  if desired

Combine all ingredients. Serve at room temperature.

Tempura Sauce

1 cup

⅛ teaspoon ground ginger
⅓ cup Japanese soy sauce
  (shoyu)
½ teaspoon sugar

⅔ cup water
2 tablespoons sake *or* dry
  sherry

Combine all ingredients. Serve in small individual bowls as a dipping sauce.

Teriyaki Sauce or Marinade

1½ cups
Marinate meat, fish or shellfish in sauce, or baste with sauce during cooking.

⅔ cup finely chopped onion
2 tablespoons sugar
1 tablespoon minced fresh ginger root *or*
2 teaspoons ground ginger
2 cloves garlic, minced

½ cup cider vinegar *or* dry white wine
⅓ cup Japanese soy sauce (shoyu)
½ teaspoon monosodium glutamate

Combine all ingredients.

Orange Sauce

(*Sauce Bigarade*) 2 cups
For game and domestic fowl, particularly duck.

½ cup red currant jelly
1 peppercorn
1½ cups brown gravy *or* canned beef gravy
Juice of 2 oranges

Grated rind of 1 orange
Grated rind of ½ lemon
1 tablespoon Madeira wine, if desired

1. In saucepan, melt jelly. Add peppercorn, ½ cup gravy, orange juice and rind and lemon rind. Bring to boil. Reduce heat. Simmer 20 minutes, or just until thickened.
2. Add remaining 1 cup brown gravy. Heat, but do not boil.
3. Strain sauce and stir in wine. Serve hot.

Sauce Verte

(*Green Mayonnaise*)   1 cup
For chilled fish and for seafood and vegetable salads.

1 cup good mayonnaise
2 hard-cooked egg yolks
2 tablespoons chopped
  parsley
2 tablespoons chopped fresh
  tarragon *or* dill

2 tablespoons chopped chives
2 tablespoons chopped raw
  spinach
1 teaspoon lemon juice

Place all ingredients in electric blender for 1 minute, or press through food mill. Serve cold.

Marinade for Chicken

⅓ cup cooking oil
⅓ cup wine vinegar
  1 small clove garlic, crushed
½ cup minced onion
  1 tablespoon Worcestershire
  sauce
½ teaspoon salt

¼ cup finely chopped celery
½ teaspoon freshly ground
  pepper
Dash liquid hot pepper sauce
½ teaspoon each dried
  oregano, thyme and
  tarragon *or* rosemary

1. Combine all ingredients.
2. Pour marinade over uncooked, disjointed chicken. Marinate in refrigerator 4 hours or overnight, turning chicken several times.
3. Baste chicken with marinade during cooking, or serve marinated cold cooked chicken on bed of lettuce.

Glaze for Baked Ham

Adds zest to canned ham, baked ham or ham slices.

½ cup firmly packed brown
  sugar
1 tablespoon dry mustard
1 tablespoon all-purpose
  flour

¼ cup vinegar
1 cup pineapple juice *or*
  hot water

1. In small mixing bowl, make paste of sugar, mustard, flour
   and vinegar. Add pineapple juice or water. Stir until
   blended and sugar is dissolved.
2. Baste ham frequently with glaze during baking.

Honey Glaze

For ham, pork and onions.

⅓ cup honey
⅓ cup soy sauce
1½ teaspoons prepared mustard

Combine all ingredients. Baste meat with sauce during cooking, or pour over cooked onions.

Apricot Stuffing

About 5 cups
Good for stuffing game or domestic birds as well as pork.
Allow 1 cup stuffing for each pound of ready-to-cook poultry
or game.

½ pound dried apricots,
cooked, drained and
chopped (reserve juice)
4 cups dried bread, cubed
½ cup chopped nutmeats
½ teaspoon salt

1 tablespoon chopped
parsley
Grated rind of 1 orange,
if desired
¼ cup melted butter

1. Combine apricots, bread cubes, nutmeats, salt, parsley and orange rind, if desired.
2. Sprinkle melted butter over mixture. Add enough reserved apricot juice to give desired moistness. Toss lightly with fork until blended.

Sherried Stuffing for Turkey

About 8 cups
Allow 1 cup stuffing for each pound of ready-to-cook turkey.

Chopped, cooked turkey
giblets
½ pound lean ground pork
¼ cup butter
¼ cup slivered almonds
½ cup white raisins
¼ cup finely chopped green
pepper
¼ cup finely chopped onion

¼ cup finely chopped
parsley
¼ cup finely chopped celery
¼ teaspoon powdered
oregano
½ cup tomato sauce
1 to 1½ cups sherry
1 teaspoon salt
¼ teaspoon paprika
4 cups bread cubes

1. In large skillet, sauté chopped giblets and pork in butter.
2. Add almonds, raisins, green pepper, onion, parsley and celery. Sauté 3 to 5 minutes more, or until vegetables are limp.

3. Remove from heat. Add remaining ingredients, tossing with fork until blended. Add more wine or water if dressing is too dry.
4. Allow to cool before stuffing bird.

Wild Rice Stuffing for Poultry and Game Birds

About 3 cups
Allow 1 cup stuffing for each pound of ready-to-cook poultry or game.

1 cup uncooked wild rice	⅛ teaspoon pepper *or*
1 medium onion, finely chopped	seasoned pepper
	1 egg, lightly beaten
¾ cup chopped celery	1 cup stock from rice *or*
1 small green pepper, finely chopped	1 can (10½ ounces) cream of mushroom soup
2 tablespoons butter	¼ cup Burgundy wine
1 teaspoon salt	

1. Wash rice thoroughly. Cook, following directions on package, adding a few minutes' cooking time. Drain. Reserve liquid, if any remains.
2. Meanwhile, in skillet, sauté onion, celery and green pepper lightly in butter. Add salt, pepper or seasoned pepper and egg. Stir well.
3. Combine cooked rice, onion mixture, stock or soup and wine. Toss with fork until blended.
4. Allow to cool before stuffing bird.

Wild Rice Stuffing with Pecans and Bacon: In Step 2, sauté 6 slices diced bacon with vegetables. Omit butter. In Step 3, add ¾ cup chopped pecan meats or halves.

Herb Stuffing for Fish

About 4 cups

1 package herb-seasoned
  stuffing (about 3½ cups)
1 teaspoon ground sage
½ teaspoon ground thyme
½ teaspoon ground rosemary
1 teaspoon salt
1 tablespoon chopped
  parsley
⅓ cup melted butter
1 cup fish broth *or* chicken
  consommé
1 tablespoon dry sherry, if
  desired
½ cup flaked crabmeat *or*
  sliced shrimp, if desired

Combine all ingredients. Toss with fork until blended. Put stuffing lightly into fish cavity or wrap fish fillets around stuffing and secure with skewer or toothpick.

Sauerkraut Stuffing

Synonymous with roast wild game birds, particularly goose. Generally used for effective flavoring, but not eating.

1 can (16 ounces) sauerkraut
1 cup chopped apple
1 cup chopped onion
¾ cup chopped celery

Combine all ingredients and stuff bird. Discard after roasting, if desired.

Salads
& Salad Dressings

Stuffed Artichoke Salad
1 serving

1 cooked artichoke
¼ cup cooked, chopped
crabmeat, shrimp *or*
lobster
1 tablespoon chopped celery
1 tablespoon chopped green
pepper

2 tablespoons Thousand
Island Dressing *or*
mayonnaise, thinned with
1 tablespoon cream
Salt
Pepper
½ teaspoon capers, caviar *or*
chopped hard-cooked egg

1. Press cooked artichoke leaves back to open out like a flower. Pull and scrape out choke in center, leaving a cup.
2. Mix crab, shrimp or lobster with celery, green pepper, dressing or mayonnaise and salt and pepper to taste. Fill artichoke center. Garnish with capers, caviar or chopped hard-cooked egg.

Artichoke Salad Plate: Omit seafood stuffing. Fill centers with this dressing: 2 tablespoons good mayonnaise, 1 teaspoon chopped chives, ½ teaspoon lemon juice and dash of salt, beaten together. Top with watercress sprig.

Party Crab Salad

6 servings

Bibb or leaf lettuce leaves
  6 slices canned pineapple
  6 large slices tomato
  1 avocado, peeled and
    sliced
  1 cup croutons, sautéed in
    butter
 24 pecan halves
1½ pounds cooked crabmeat,
    picked over and cut in
    bite-size pieces

2 cups good mayonnaise
½ cup dairy sour cream
1 can (No. 2½) pear
  halves, drained and
  diced
2 to 3 teaspoons diced
  cucumber
1 teaspoon diced onion
1 teaspoon diced celery
Parsley

1. For each salad, make bed of lettuce leaves. Place a slice each of pineapple, tomato and avocado on lettuce. Sprinkle with croutons, pecan halves and one-sixth of crabmeat.
2. In mixing bowl, combine remaining ingredients. Pour over salads and garnish with additional parsley.

Cottage Cheese Salad

6 to 8 servings

 1 tablespoon unflavored
  gelatin
¼ cup water
 2 cups small-curd cottage
  cheese
½ cup crumbled Roquefort
  cheese
 1 teaspoon salt

⅛ teaspoon paprika
½ cup cream
12 sliced stuffed olives
¼ cup chopped nutmeats
Watercress *or* lettuce
Mayonnaise *or* Thousand
  Island Dressing
Chopped parsley

1. In custard-size cup, soften gelatin in water. Place over simmering water until dissolved.
2. In mixing bowl, beat together cheeses, salt, paprika and cream, until smooth. Stir in olives and nutmeats. Add gelatin.
3. Pour into lightly oiled 1-quart mold. Chill 4 hours, or until set.
4. Unmold, garnish with watercress or lettuce and serve with Mayonnaise or Thousand Island Dressing, sprinkled with chopped parsley.

Cranberry Wine Mold

6 servings

1 medium orange, washed
¾ cup port wine
2 whole cloves
Dash ground cinnamon
1 package (3 ounces) raspberry *or* cherry gelatin

1 can (1 pound) whole cranberry sauce
1 cup chopped pecan meats
1 cup dairy sour cream
Pecan halves

1. Grind orange.
2. In small saucepan, combine ground orange, wine, cloves and cinnamon. Bring to boil. Reduce heat. Simmer 3 minutes. Remove from heat. Remove cloves.
3. Dissolve gelatin in hot spiced wine. Add cranberry sauce and chopped pecan meats.
4. Pour into lightly oiled 1½-quart mold. Refrigerate until set.
5. Unmold and frost with sour cream and garnish with pecan halves. Or serve plain, passing sour cream as sauce.

Frosted Fruit Gelatin

10 to 12 servings

1 package (3 ounces) orange gelatin
1 package (3 ounces) lemon gelatin
2 cups boiling water
1½ cups cold water
1 can (No. 2) crushed pineapple and juice
1 can (11 ounces) mandarin oranges, drained
2 large bananas

40 miniature marshmallows
½ cup sugar
2 tablespoons all-purpose flour
1 egg, beaten
1 cup pineapple juice
1 tablespoon orange juice
2 tablespoons butter *or* margarine
1 cup whipping cream, whipped

1. Dissolve gelatins in boiling water. Add cold water. Stir in undrained pineapple and drained mandarin oranges.
2. Pour into large shallow dish or pan. Slice bananas over top of gelatin. Arrange marshmallows between banana slices. Refrigerate until set.
3. Make topping: Combine remaining ingredients, except whipped cream, in medium-size saucepan. Cook over medium-low heat until thickened. Cool. Spread on set gelatin. Refrigerate.
4. Frost with whipped cream. Cut into squares to serve.

Spanish Tuna-Fish Salad or Spread

1 cup

A savory spread for crisp crackers, to serve with cocktails or sherry; or served as a salad on lettuce leaves.

1 can (6 or 7 ounces)
  albacore tuna, drained
1 tablespoon olive oil
2 tablespoons dry sherry

1 small onion, minced
2 tablespoons finely chopped
  parsley
Dash paprika

Mix all ingredients together, tossing lightly but well. Chill thoroughly before serving.

Shrimp Mousse
About 10 servings

1 cup condensed tomato
  soup
2 tablespoons unflavored
  gelatin
3 packages (3 ounces each)
  cream cheese, softened
1 can (7 ounces) shrimp,
  drained and finely
  chopped

1 cup good mayonnaise
½ cup water
1 cup finely chopped onion
1 cup finely chopped celery
1 cup finely chopped green
  pepper

1. In saucepan, heat soup. Stir in gelatin and softened cheese. Cool.
2. Add remaining ingredients. Pour into 2-quart ring mold. Refrigerate until firm.
3. Turn out onto bed of lettuce or other greens.

Gorgonzola Cheese Dressing

About 2½ cups
Roquefort or blue cheese may be substituted for Gorgonzola.

1 pound Gorgonzola cheese,
    crumbled
⅓ cup half-and-half cream

1 teaspoon chopped parsley
1 teaspoon lemon juice
1 cup good mayonnaise

1. In mixing bowl, stir and beat cheese until creamy.
2. Gradually add cream. Add remaining ingredients. Mix well.
3. Chill before serving. Stored in refrigerator, this keeps well.

Old-fashioned Dressing for Coleslaw

About 1½ cups
Keeps indefinitely in a tightly covered container in the refrigerator. This is a prize-winning recipe.

½ cup white vinegar
½ cup water
3 tablespoons sugar
1 teaspoon salt
1 tablespoon butter *or*
    margarine

1 tablespoon all-purpose
    flour
¼ teaspoon dry mustard
1 egg

1. In small saucepan combine vinegar, water, sugar, salt and butter or margarine. Bring to boil over medium heat.
2. Mix together flour, mustard and egg. Add to hot mixture. Cook, stirring constantly, until thickened.
3. If too thick, add a little milk. Chill before using.

Vinaigrette Dressing I

1½ cups

Serve vinaigrette dressings over cooked or uncooked vege-tables, over green or mixed-vegetable salads, and use as a marinade for hors d'oeuvres.

¾ cup olive oil
½ cup tarragon wine vinegar
¾ teaspoon salt
¼ teaspoon freshly ground
    pepper

2 teaspoons finely chopped
    chives
⅛ teaspoon dried chervil
2 teaspoons minced capers
1 hard-cooked egg yolk,
    mashed

Beat all ingredients well together.

Vinaigrette Dressing II

1½ cups

1 cup olive oil
⅓ cup wine vinegar
½ teaspoon salt
¼ teaspoon freshly ground
    pepper

1 teaspoon chopped shallots
1 teaspoon prepared
    mustard
1 teaspoon chopped parsley,
    if desired

Combine all ingredients. Blend well.

Vegetables

Hawaiian Vegetable Tempura

6 servings

Vegetables may be prepared, wrapped, and stored in refrigerator until time to cook.

1 pound artichoke hearts,
  green beans, eggplant,
  large mushrooms, turnip
  slices, asparagus tips or
  green pepper
1 cup water

1 teaspoon double-acting
  baking powder
1 cup sifted all-purpose flour
Cooking oil *or* shortening
Tempura Sauce, page 162

1. Wash vegetables and cut into 2-inch lengths. Cut eggplant in half lengthwise, then into ½-inch thick pieces.
2. In mixing bowl combine water, baking powder and flour. Beat until smooth.
3. In large cooking pan or deep-fat fryer, heat oil or shortening to 350° to 360°F. Have sufficient oil or shortening to float vegetables—it should be at least 1½ inches deep.
4. Dip vegetables in batter.
5. Fry until light brown. Turn over once. Do not overcook.
6. Serve hot with Tempura Sauce.

Green Beans with Dill

4 servings

1 pound green beans,
cooked and drained
2 tablespoons butter
½ teaspoon salt

1 package (3 ounces) cream
cheese, softened
2 to 3 tablespoons coffee
cream
1 teaspoon dried dill seed

Combine all ingredients, tossing to blend flavors. Heat through. Serve immediately.

Artichokes Italiana

4 servings

4 large artichokes, washed
½ bunch parsley, washed and
shaken dry
12 cloves garlic

1 cup olive oil
Hot water
1 teaspoon salt

1. Remove small outer leaves around bottoms of artichokes and ½ inch of bottom stem. If desired, cut off spiny tips of leaves. Invert artichokes and push down on them to open out all leaves. Break parsley into clusters and stud artichoke center and between leaves with parsley sprigs.
2. Remove outer skin from garlic cloves and cut each into about 3 slices. Tuck 8 to 10 garlic slices among leaves of each artichoke.
3. Place artichokes close together in pan just large enough to hold them. Pour in olive oil. Marinate in oil 10 minutes.

4. Add hot water to cover and sprinkle with salt.
5. Boil for 30 minutes, or until tender.
6. If pressure cooker is used, cook 10 minutes at 15 pounds pressure. (See Pressure Cooker, page 13, for additional information, altitude and time adjustments.) Cool cooker quickly in cold water.
7. Drain and serve hot as a vegetable, or at room temperature as a first course.

Asparagus Parmigiana

6 servings

A delicious treatment for a vegetable that was so prized in Roman times that it was taken by chariots to the Alps where it was frozen to preserve it.

2 pounds lightly cooked asparagus spears, drained
1 medium onion, finely chopped
1 clove garlic, minced
3 tablespoons butter
¾ teaspoon salt
Dash liquid hot pepper sauce

1 can (1 pound) tomatoes
¼ teaspoon powdered thyme
1 can (8 ounces) tomato sauce
½ pound grated mozzarella cheese
Grated Parmesan cheese
Buttered Bread Crumbs, page 75

1. Preheat oven to 350°F. Butter shallow baking dish.
2. Arrange drained asparagus in baking dish.
3. In skillet, sauté onion and garlic in butter until limp. Add salt, liquid hot pepper sauce and tomatoes. Simmer 10 minutes, stirring frequently. Add thyme and tomato sauce. Simmer 20 minutes more.

4. Pour sauce over asparagus. Sprinkle with mozzarella cheese. Sprinkle lightly with Parmesan cheese and Buttered Bread Crumbs.
5. Bake 20 minutes, or just until cheeses are bubbly and top is golden brown.

Sweet and Sour Red Cabbage

6 to 8 servings

1 large head red cabbage	½ cup cider vinegar
¾ cup applesauce	1 cup water
¾ cup sugar	

1. Remove core from cabbage and cut into ¾-inch slices. Place in large crock or stainless steel pan. Add applesauce, sugar, cider vinegar, and water. Mix well.
2. Let marinate in cool place or refrigerator overnight.
3. Cook over medium heat until tender. Serve hot.

Stuffed Green Peppers

6 servings

6 medium green peppers, tops cut off, seeds and membrane removed	¾ cup rice
1 pound ground beef	1 tablespoon Worcestershire sauce
1 small onion, chopped	½ teaspoon seasoned salt
1 tablespoon cooking oil	⅛ teaspoon seasoned pepper
1 can (1 pound) stewed tomatoes	1 cup grated mild Cheddar cheese

1. In large heavy saucepan, parboil peppers 5 minutes. Drain.
2. In skillet, brown beef and onion in cooking oil, chopping meat into small granules. Add stewed tomatoes, rice, Worcestershire sauce, seasoned salt and pepper. Cover. Simmer 5 minutes. Stir in cheese.
3. Stuff peppers with meat mixture. Place in lightly greased baking dish. Add ¼ cup water, if desired.
4. Bake at 350°F. for 30 to 40 minutes.

Cheese Stuffed Peppers: In Step 2, substitute cottage cheese for meat stuffing. Cover peppers with canned tomato sauce.

Shrimp Stuffed Peppers: In Step 2, make stuffing of 2 cups cooked, diced shrimp, 1½ cups cooked rice, ½ teaspoon instant minced onion, and 1 cup good mayonnaise. Pour canned tomato sauce around peppers during baking.

Beets in Orange Sauce

4 to 6 servings

¼ cup sugar
 1 tablespoon cornstarch
 1 teaspoon salt
½ cup orange juice
 1 teaspoon grated orange rind

3 tablespoons butter *or* margarine
½ cup dairy sour cream
 3 cups cooked, drained beets

1. In 1-quart saucepan, mix sugar, cornstarch, and salt together. Add orange juice and rind. Cook over low heat until thickened and clear, stirring constantly.
2. Add butter or margarine and beets. Cook over low heat for about 15 minutes, stirring occasionally.
3. Stir in sour cream and reheat to a simmer; do not boil.

Broccoli with Tuna Fish Sauce

4 servings

1 package (10 ounces)
   frozen broccoli spears,
   cooked and drained
1 can (7½ ounces) tuna fish,
   drained and flaked
1 can (10½ ounces) cream
   of mushroom soup
¾ cup good mayonnaise

1 teaspoon curry powder
1 tablespoon lemon juice
¼ teaspoon pepper
1 teaspoon chopped
   pimiento, if desired
Buttered Bread Crumbs,
   page 75

1. Preheat oven to 350°F. Butter 1½-quart casserole.
2. Arrange cooked and drained broccoli in bottom of prepared casserole. Cover with tuna fish.
3. Combine remaining ingredients. Pour over tuna fish.
   Sprinkle with Buttered Bread Crumbs.
4. Bake for 30 minutes, or until bubbly and brown.

Carrots with Herbs

4 servings

1 pound carrots
1 cup boiling water
1½ teaspoons salt
¼ teaspoon dried sweet
   basil

¼ teaspoon dried marjoram
¼ teaspoon dried savory
3 tablespoons butter
Dash seasoned pepper, if
   desired

1. Wash and scrape carrots. Cut into quarters lengthwise,
   then into halves crosswise.

2. Cook carrots in salted boiling water to cover for 25 to 30 minutes, or until tender. Drain. Add remaining ingredients. Heat through; or place under broiler until heated through.

Celery with Pecans

6 servings

5 cups chopped celery
1 teaspoon salt
1 cup boiling water
2 cups Medium White
Sauce, page 155

1 cup chopped pecan meats
½ teaspoon crumbled sweet
basil
Buttered Bread Crumbs,
page 75

1. In medium-size saucepan, cook celery in salted boiling water until almost done, about 20 minutes. Drain well.
2. Preheat oven to 375°F. Butter 1½-quart casserole.
3. Spoon drained celery into casserole.
4. Combine White Sauce, pecan meats, and sweet basil. Pour over celery. Sprinkle with Buttered Bread Crumbs.
5. Bake for 30 minutes, or until heated through and bubbly.

Corn Pudding

6 servings

2 cups corn, cut from the
cob *or* 2 cups whole-
kernel canned corn,
drained
⅛ teaspoon ground nutmeg
1 teaspoon salt
⅛ teaspoon seasoned salt

⅛ teaspoon seasoned pepper
2 teaspoons sugar
3 eggs, slightly beaten
2 tablespoons butter *or*
margarine
2 cups milk

1. Preheat oven to 325°F. Butter 2-quart casserole.
2. In mixing bowl, combine corn, nutmeg, salts, pepper and sugar. Add eggs. Mix well.
3. In small saucepan, heat butter or margarine with milk until melted. Blend into corn mixture.
4. Spoon into prepared casserole.
5. Place in shallow pan on oven rack. Pour boiling water into pan to depth of 1 inch.
6. Bake for 1 hour, or until a knife inserted in center of custard comes out clean.

Baked Eggplant

6 servings

1 medium eggplant	½ cup dry bread crumbs
2 tablespoons finely chopped onion	1 teaspoon lemon juice
	Salt
2 tablespoons bacon drippings	Pepper *or* seasoned pepper

1. Boil whole eggplant in water to cover for 30 minutes. Cool, peel and chop into small cubes.
2. Preheat oven to 350°F. Butter 1½-quart casserole.
3. In small skillet, sauté onions in bacon drippings until limp. Add bread crumbs. Sauté 2 minutes more.
4. Combine eggplant, bread and onion mixture, lemon juice and salt and pepper to taste. Spoon into buttered casserole.
5. Bake at 350°F. until heated through and lightly browned, about 20 minutes.

Sautéed Cucumber Wedges

6 servings

3 slender cucumbers, peeled
and cut into ½-inch
wedges lengthwise
3 tablespoons butter

½ teaspoon monosodium
glutamate
1 teaspoon chopped parsley
Salt
Seasoned pepper

1. In skillet, melt butter and sauté cucumbers just until well heated through.
2. Add monosodium glutamate, parsley and salt and seasoned pepper to taste. Stir to blend all flavors and cook a moment or two more, or until golden. Do not allow cucumbers to brown.

Braised Lettuce

4 servings

4 medium heads Boston
lettuce
1 can (10½ ounces) chicken
consommé
½ cup water

¼ teaspoon instant minced
onion
Salt
Pepper
Chopped parsley

1. In large saucepan with cover, bring enough water to cover lettuce to *furious* boil.
2. Wash lettuce. Remove wilted outside leaves. Rewash. Drain. Cut in quarters.
3. Place in boiling water. Cover. Boil just until tender, about 10 minutes. Drain.

4. Place lettuce in 1½-quart baking dish. Cover with consommé, water, minced onion and salt and pepper to taste. Sprinkle with chopped parsley.
5. Bake at 350°F. for about 30 minutes, or until lettuce has thoroughly absorbed seasonings.

French Leeks

6 servings

3 large *or* 6 small leeks, cut in half lengthwise	1 cup beef bouillon *or* stock
	¼ cup dry white wine
1 tablespoon butter	1 tablespoon minced parsley

1. In skillet with cover, sauté leeks in butter until pale gold and limp. Add bouillon and wine. Cover.
2. Cook until tender, about 35 to 40 minutes. Sprinkle with parsley.

Creamed Mushrooms

4 servings
Serve over hot toast points, in patty shells, or as a supreme sauce for such cooked vegetables as green beans or peas.

1 pound fresh mushrooms	1½ cups milk
1 tablespoon butter	½ teaspoon salt
2 teaspoons minced onion	⅛ teaspoon pepper
4 teaspoons all-purpose flour	1 teaspoon lemon juice
	¾ teaspoon celery salt

1. Wash mushrooms, if necessary, and dry; or wipe with a damp cloth. Slice lengthwise or halve, according to size.
2. In medium-size skillet over low heat, melt butter. Add onions. Cover. Cook for 10 minutes.
3. Add prepared mushrooms. Re-cover and sauté for 10 minutes, stirring occasionally. Sprinkle with flour and blend in. Add milk and blend. Cook over low heat, stirring constantly, until thickened. Add salt, pepper, lemon juice and celery salt. Blend well. Serve piping hot.

Baked Stuffed Onions

4 servings

4 medium Bermuda onions	2 tablespoons chopped
2 tablespoons butter	celery
1 cup soft bread crumbs	1 teaspoon salt
¼ cup chopped pecan meats	Dash cayenne pepper
2 tablespoons chopped	Grated Parmesan cheese
parsley	Water

1. Cook onions in boiling salted water until almost tender. Drain. Remove centers of onions without disturbing outer shell. Chop onion centers fine.
2. In skillet, sauté chopped onion in butter for 2 or 3 minutes. Add bread crumbs, pecan meats, parsley, celery, salt and cayenne pepper.
3. Stuff onions with mixture. Sprinkle with Parmesan cheese.
4. Place stuffed onions in shallow baking dish. Add ¼ cup hot water.
5. Bake at 400°F. for 30 minutes, or until golden brown.

Baked Stuffed Tomatoes with Rice

6 servings

6 medium tomatoes, washed	½ teaspoon salt
2 teaspoons minced onion	⅛ teaspoon pepper
2 teaspoons finely chopped green pepper	½ cup Buttered Bread Crumbs, page 75
2 tablespoons butter	¼ teaspoon crushed dried sweet basil
1 cup cooked rice	

1. Preheat oven to 350°F. Have ready shallow baking dish.
2. Cut ½-inch slice off top of stem end of each tomato. Scoop out pulp. Drain shell upside down on paper toweling.
3. In medium skillet over low heat, sauté onions and green pepper in butter until limp. Add rice, salt and pepper. Stir until well blended.
4. Fill tomato cavities with rice mixture. Place stuffed tomatoes in baking dish.
5. Bake 20 minutes. Remove from oven. Top with Buttered Bread Crumbs mixed with basil.
6. Heat under broiler until golden brown.

Cherry Tomatoes Sauté

6 servings

1 shallot, sliced	3 cups cherry tomatoes, washed and stems removed
2 small onions, peeled, sliced and separated into rings	1 teaspoon sugar
½ teaspoon dried sweet basil	½ teaspoon salt
3 tablespoons butter	1 tablespoon dry sherry

1. In medium-size skillet, sauté shallot, onions and basil in melted butter until limp.
2. Add tomatoes. Sprinkle with sugar, salt and sherry. Cook, tossing lightly, just until tomato skins begin to pop, about 3 minutes. Serve at once.

Parsnip Patties

6 servings

2 cups mashed cooked parsnips	1 teaspoon lemon juice
1 teaspoon salt	⅛ teaspoon ground allspice
½ teaspoon seasoned salt	1 egg, beaten
¼ teaspoon seasoned pepper	½ cup fine, dry bread crumbs
1 teaspoon sugar	Flour
½ teaspoon paprika	Bacon drippings

1. In mixing bowl, combine all ingredients except flour and bacon drippings. Toss lightly but well.
2. Shape into 6 patties. Dredge in flour.
3. In skillet, melt bacon drippings and sauté patties, turning once. Serve hot.

Turnip Patties: Substitute turnips for parsnips. Substitute ½ teaspoon crumbled sweet basil for sugar.

Peas in Wine Sauce

6 servings

2 pounds fresh peas, shelled, *or* 2 packages (10 ounces each) frozen tiny peas
1 cup very thinly sliced celery
1 teaspoon seasoned salt
1 teaspoon monosodium glutamate

1 cup chicken consommé
¼ cup dry white wine
4 tablespoons butter
⅛ teaspoon seasoned pepper
1 tablespoon chopped parsley
2 to 3 teaspoons cornstarch, if desired

1. In saucepan with cover, combine peas, celery, salt, monosodium glutamate and consommé. Bring to boil. Cover. Cook over medium heat until peas are tender.
2. Add wine, butter, pepper and parsley.
3. Mix cornstarch with a little water. Add to peas. Stir well and cook until sauce has thickened and flavors are blended.

Chinese Snow Pea Pods with Water Chestnuts

4 servings

1 package (8 ounces) frozen pea pods, *or* 8 ounces fresh pea pods
2 cups chicken stock

9 canned water chestnuts, thinly sliced
1½ tablespoons cornstarch

1. If using fresh pea pods, snap off both ends and remove the string from the back of the pods.

2. In saucepan, bring chicken stock to boil. Add pea pods to stock. Simmer gently for about 15 minutes. Add sliced water chestnuts. Thicken with cornstarch mixed with a little cold water. Stir well and cook until sauce has thickened and flavors are blended.

Potato Casserole

4 to 6 servings

5 to 6 medium potatoes	1 teaspoon salt
2 tablespoons butter	2 shallots *or* green onions,
1½ tablespoons all-purpose	finely chopped
flour	5 tablespoons grated
1½ cups potato water *or*	cheese
chicken or vegetable	Bread crumbs
stock	

1. Peel and slice potatoes. Cover with water. Cook until tender but not mushy. Remove from heat. Drain, reserving potato water.
2. Preheat oven to 375°F.
3. In small saucepan over low heat, melt 1 tablespoon butter. Add flour, stirring constantly until smooth. Gradually add potato water or chicken or vegetable stock, salt and shallots or onions. Cook until thickened. Remove from heat.
4. Butter 1½-quart casserole. Put a layer of potatoes on bottom. Cover with sauce. Repeat until all of potatoes and sauce are in casserole, ending with sauce. Sprinkle grated cheese over top, then bread crumbs. Dot with remaining 1 tablespoon butter.
4. Bake at 375°F. until heated through and browned on top.

Hashed Brown Potatoes with Nectarines

6 servings

3 cups peeled, diced raw
potatoes
Cooking oil, margarine *or*
bacon drippings
½ cup finely chopped onion
¾ teaspoon salt
½ teaspoon monosodium
glutamate

¼ teaspoon white pepper
⅛ teaspoon ground turmeric
1 tablespoon lemon juice
¼ cup finely chopped
parsley
2 cups pitted, diced
nectarines

1. In large skillet over medium heat, fry potatoes in cooking oil, margarine or bacon drippings for 8 minutes. Add onion, salt, monosodium glutamate, pepper, turmeric and lemon juice. Continue cooking, turning to brown potatoes evenly, until tender, about 15 minutes.
2. Stir in parsley and nectarines. Heat through, about 5 minutes.

Fried Zucchini

8 servings

8 medium zucchini squash,
washed and peeled
2 teaspoons salt
2 tablespoons butter *or*
margarine
1 small onion, minced

2 teaspoons all-purpose
flour
¼ teaspoon paprika
¼ teaspoon sugar
1 teaspoon vinegar
1 teaspoon dried dill seed

1. Cut washed and peeled squash into 3-inch strips. Place in bowl. Add water just to cover and ½ teaspoon salt. Let stand 30 minutes. Drain. Dry on paper toweling.
2. In large skillet with cover, melt butter or margarine. Sauté squash strips and onion over medium-low heat until golden brown, stirring frequently.
3. Sprinkle with flour. Stir until well blended. Add remaining 1½ teaspoons salt, paprika, sugar, vinegar and dill seed. Cover. Cook, stirring frequently, for about 20 minutes, or until squash is tender. Add a little water, if necessary.

Tomato Zucchini: In Step 3, substitute ¼ teaspoon dried marjoram for dill. Add dash of garlic powder and 1 can (8 ounces) tomato sauce or 1 cup chopped fresh tomatoes.

Desserts
& Dessert Sauces,
Pies & Fruits

Blueberry Supreme
About 6 servings

CRUST

1¼ cups sifted all-purpose flour
 2 tablespoons sugar
 ½ cup butter

1. Preheat oven to 400°F. Have ready a 9-inch pan or baking dish.
2. Into small mixing bowl, sift flour and sugar together. With two table knives or a pastry blender, cut butter into dry ingredients until mixture resembles small grain.
3. Press dough into bottom of pan or baking dish with fingers. Bake for 25 minutes. While baking prepare filling:

FILLING

Follow directions for Soft Vanilla Custard, page 197. Add 3 tablespoons flour with eggs in Step 1. Cool. Pour into baked crust.

BLUEBERRY TOPPING

6 tablespoons granulated
  sugar
3 tablespoons cornstarch
⅛ teaspoon salt
1 cup blueberry juice
2 teaspoons butter

4 cups (two No. 2 cans)
  drained blueberries
2 teaspoons lemon juice
1 cup whipping cream,
  whipped

1. In saucepan, mix sugar, cornstarch and salt together. Gradually add blueberry juice. Cook over low heat, stirring constantly, until thickened and clear; do not undercook.
2. Add butter, blueberries and lemon juice.
3. Remove from heat. Pour over custard filling. Top with whipped cream.

Meringue Shell International

6 individual shells or one 9-inch shell
Meringues are particularly successful at high altitudes. You needn't worry about their becoming soggy or beady.

3 egg whites
⅛ teaspoon *fresh* cream of
  tartar
¼ teaspoon salt
1 teaspoon vanilla extract
1 teaspoon vinegar
1 teaspoon water
¾ cup sifted sugar

¾ cup finely chopped
  walnut meats, if desired
Fresh fruit *or* Cream
  Custard Filling, page 256,
  or Whipped Cream
  Frosting, Filling and
  Topping, page 250, *or*
  Ice cream

1. Preheat oven to 275°F. Lightly butter and flour a 9-inch pie plate or spring-form pan.
2. In medium-size mixing bowl, beat egg whites until frothy. Add cream of tartar and salt. Beat egg whites until stiff but not dry. Mix vanilla extract, vinegar and water together. Gradually add sugar to egg whites a small spoonful at a time, alternately with a few drops of liquid. With a pliable rubber scraper or whisk, gently fold in nutmeats, if desired.
3. Spread meringue in prepared pie plate or pan, building up sides to shape a nest or shell.
4. Bake 1 hour. Fill cooled shell or shells with fresh fruit, or one of the suggested fillings.

Crème Caramel

8 to 10 servings

1 cup plus 7 tablespoons sugar	1 teaspoon vanilla *or* lemon extract
10 eggs	Whipped cream
4 cups half-and-half cream	Fresh strawberries
¾ teaspoon salt	

1. Preheat oven to 300°F.
2. Over low heat, melt 1 cup sugar in 2-quart mold until golden brown. Remove from heat. Coat inside of mold by swishing caramelized sugar around sides.
3. In large mixing bowl, beat eggs slightly. Add 4 tablespoons sugar. Beat well. Add remaining 3 tablespoons sugar. Beat well. Add cream, salt and vanilla or lemon extract. Mix thoroughly. Pour into mold.

4. Place mold in shallow pan on oven rack. Pour boiling water into pan to depth of 1 inch.
5. Bake for 1½ to 2 hours, or until a silver knife inserted in center comes out clean. Cool. Refrigerate overnight.
6. Unmold. Serve with whipped cream and garnish with fresh strawberries.

Lemon Sponge

4 to 6 servings

2 eggs, separated (beat whites until stiff, but not dry)	2 tablespoons all-purpose flour
1 cup sugar	2 tablespoons melted butter
¼ teaspoon salt	Juice of 1 lemon
	Grated rind of 1 lemon
	1 cup milk

1. Preheat oven to 350°F. Butter 1-quart casserole or baking dish.
2. In mixing bowl, beat egg yolks until lemon colored. Add sugar and salt. Beat well. Add flour, melted butter, lemon juice and rind. Mix well. Gradually add milk.
3. With pliable rubber scraper or whisk, gently fold in stiffly beaten egg whites.
4. Pour into prepared casserole or baking dish. Place in shallow pan on oven rack. Pour boiling water into pan to depth of 1 inch.
5. Bake for 25 minutes, or until knife inserted in center comes out clean.

Soft Vanilla Custard

4 to 6 servings
You may find you prefer a quality, heavy saucepan and a watchful eye to a double boiler.

¼ cup sugar
¼ teaspoon salt
  2 eggs *or* 3 egg yolks,
   slightly beaten
¼ teaspoon ground
   nutmeg, if desired

1½ cups milk
  1 teaspoon vanilla extract,
   rum *or* sherry; *or* a little
   grated lemon rind

1. In top of double boiler, or in heavy 1-quart saucepan, mix together sugar, salt, eggs or egg yolks, and nutmeg, if desired. Stir in milk. Mix very well.
2. Cook over simmering water or low heat, stirring frequently, until custard coats a metal spoon. It should be slightly thicker than unbeaten egg whites.
3. Remove from heat. Add flavoring of choice. Strain. Refrigerate.

Easy Orange Soufflé

One hostess we know satisfied her curiosity about this soufflé's cooking process by purchasing a glass double boiler.

For each serving:
1 egg white
1 tablespoon powdered *or* granulated sugar
1 tablespoon orange marmalade
Soft Vanilla Custard, page 197

1. Generously butter top of a 1-quart double boiler.
2. In mixing bowl, beat egg whites until stiff but not dry. Gradually beat in sugar.
3. Chop marmalade to a pulp in blender or with sharp knife. With a pliable rubber scraper or whisk, fold marmalade gently into egg whites.
4. Pour batter into prepared pan. Cover top with waxed paper and put on lid. Have enough boiling water in bottom of double boiler to last for 1 hour without adding to it. Place top of double boiler over bottom. Cook for 1 hour without peeking over heat that will keep water at a low boil. Serve with Soft Vanilla Custard, using the remaining egg yolks to make custard.

Orange Trifle

4 to 6 servings

Soft Vanilla Custard,
  page 197
12 ladyfingers, split in half
  lengthwise
¼ cup orange marmalade

2 tablespoons sweet sherry
½ cup whipping cream,
  whipped
Ground nutmeg

1. Prepare and cool custard. Have ready a glass serving dish.
2. Spread ladyfinger halves with marmalade. Put them back together.
3. Arrange layer of ladyfingers in bottom of dish; sprinkle with sherry. Spoon custard over ladyfingers. Repeat process until all ladyfingers have been used. Pour all remaining custard over last layer. Refrigerate overnight.
4. Before serving, spread with whipped cream. Sprinkle with nutmeg.

Ideal Pudding

8 to 10 servings

1 tablespoon unflavored
 gelatin
¾ cup water
2½ cups milk
⅞ cup sugar
1 teaspoon salt

1 teaspoon vanilla extract
1 cup whipping cream,
 whipped
3 egg whites, beaten until
 stiff but not dry
Butterscotch Sauce, page 202

1. Soak gelatin in water for 5 minutes.
2. In saucepan, scald 1 cup milk. Add sugar, salt and gelatin. Stir until completely dissolved. Add 1½ cups cold milk. Refrigerate until consistency of egg whites.
3. Butter a 2-quart mold or individual molds or cups.
4. When milk mixture is consistency of egg whites, beat with rotary beater or electric mixer until light and fluffy. Add vanilla extract.
5. With rubber scraper or whisk, fold in whipped cream and stiffly beaten egg whites. Pour into prepared large mold or individual molds or cups.
6. Refrigerate until firm. Unmold and serve with Butterscotch Sauce.

Steamed Pudding

About 8 servings

This is called Ohio Pudding, Carrot Pudding, and even Plum Pudding. Many cooks prefer to steam puddings in the pressure cooker at high altitudes, as it saves time and eliminates the need for frequent additions of water to the kettle.

¾ cup sifted all-purpose
    flour
¾ cup firmly packed brown
    sugar
½ teaspoon baking soda
¼ teaspoon salt
½ teaspoon ground
    cinnamon
½ teaspoon ground nutmeg

½ teaspoon ground cloves
½ cup grated raw carrot
½ cup grated raw potato
½ cup melted shortening
½ cup raisins
¾ cup chopped cranberries
½ cup chopped nutmeats
½ cup shredded coconut, if
    desired

1. Grease two 1-pound coffee cans or a 1½quart mold.
2. Sift flour, sugar, soda, salt, cinnamon, nutmeg and cloves together into large mixing bowl.
3. Add carrot, potato, shortening, raisins, cranberries, nutmeats and coconut, if desired.
4. Spoon batter into prepared coffee cans or mold. Cover. Set on a trivet or rack in a deep kettle. Add enough boiling water to reach halfway up mold. Steam for 3 hours, tightly covered. Replenish water as necessary, using boiling water.

Pressure-Cooker Steamed Pudding: In Step 4, place filled cans or mold on rack in pressure cooker. Add 6 cups water. Cover. Cook without gauge, allowing steam to escape for 15 minutes. Replace gauge and cook at 15 pounds pressure at 5,000 feet for 40 minutes. Reduce pressure quickly by cooling cooker in cold water. (See Pressure Cooker, page 13, for additional information, altitude and time adjustment.) Remove covers from cans or mold. Bake in oven preheated to 350°F. for 5 minutes to dry out top.

Frozen Fruit Dessert

8 servings

1½ cups crushed vanilla
    wafers
¼ cup melted butter
2 tablespoons orange juice
1 tablespoon lemon juice
20 large marshmallows,
    cut up

1 cup crushed fresh well-
    drained fruit: peaches,
    raspberries, strawberries,
    blackberries, apricots,
    oranges *or* blueberries
1 cup whipping cream,
    whipped

1. Lightly butter 8 x 2 x 8-inch square pan. Mix vanilla wafer crumbs with melted butter. Press evenly over pan bottom and sides.
2. In 1-quart saucepan, bring orange and lemon juice to boil over low heat. Add marshmallows. Stir until dissolved. Cool.
3. With pliable rubber scraper, fold fruit and whipped cream into marshmallow mixture. Spread over crumbs. Freeze 3 to 4 hours, or until firm.
4. Cut into squares to serve.

Unique Dessert Topping

About 1½ cups

This sauce keeps several days in the refrigerator. Equally suited to fresh or canned fruits and to cake slices, it is fascinating on chocolate or coffee ice cream.

8 to 10 dry coconut
    macaroons
1 tablespoon brown sugar
½ cup cream sherry

1 cup dairy sour
    cream
3 tablespoons chopped,
    toasted almonds

1. In mixing bowl, crumble macaroons into very small pieces. Add sugar and sherry. Let stand 30 minutes.
2. Add sour cream and nuts. Blend well. Chill at least 2 hours before serving.

Butterscotch Sauce
About 2½ cups

1¼ cups firmly packed brown sugar
⅔ cup light corn syrup

4 tablespoons butter
⅔ cup coffee cream

1. In heavy saucepan, combine sugar, corn syrup and butter. Bring to boil over low heat.
2. Cook, stirring constantly, until a small quantity dropped into cold water forms a soft ball. Gradually add cream. Remove from heat.

Pie baking is affected by high altitude because of the faster rate of evaporation of liquid and the "drying out" of flour. In either case, a little additional liquid is the remedy.

Fruit and berry pies require additional baking time, but with time and slight temperature adjustments, sea-level recipes for pies and pastries generally work successfully at higher elevations.

Crumb Crust for Pies

Graham Cracker Crust for 8- or 9-inch Pie Shell:
1⅓ cups graham cracker crumbs (about 16 crackers)
¼ cup melted butter *or* margarine
⅓ cup sugar

Cookie Crust for 8- or 9-inch Pie Shell:
1⅓ cups cookie crumbs (about 20 to 24 vanilla or chocolate wafers *or* gingersnaps)
6 tablespoons softened butter *or* margarine

1. Make crumbs by mashing crackers or cookies with potato masher, or by breaking into blender and blending on medium speed, inverting container occasionally to reverse crumbs and unblended pieces, or roll out with rolling pin on bread board or between sheets of waxed paper.
2. In medium-size mixing bowl, mix crumbs with sugar and melted butter, or melt butter in pie plate and add crumbs and sugar.

3. Reserve 2 tablespoons crumbs to sprinkle on top of pie, if desired. Press crumbs with back of spoon or fork tines into bottom and sides of 8- or 9-inch pie plate, forming slight rim.
4. Refrigerate before filling, or bake in oven preheated to 375°F. for 10 to 15 minutes. Cool before filling.

Basic Pastry for Pies

One-crust 8- or 9-inch Pie Shell:
1 cup sifted all-purpose flour
½ teaspoon salt
⅓ cup shortening (hydrogenated, emulsified or lard)
2½ tablespoons water

Two-crust 8- or 9-inch Pie:
2 cups sifted all-purpose flour
1 teaspoon salt
⅔ cup shortening (hydrogenated, emulsified or lard)
5 tablespoons water

1. Sift flour and salt into medium-size mixing bowl. Add shortening.
2. With two table knives or pastry blender, cut shortening into flour until consistency of small grain. Sprinkle few drops of water or liquid over flour mixture. Quickly blend by tossing pastry dough with few light strokes of fork. Add remaining water or liquid a little at a time and repeat blending with fork.
3. With loosely cupped hands, gently form pastry into two balls, making one a little larger than the other. This is one of the secrets of flaky pastry, as the more you handle the pastry dough, the tougher it gets. *Do not roll or pack dough in palms of hands.*
4. On lightly floured surface, or between two 12-inch squares

of waxed paper, or on pastry canvas, place the larger ball
of dough to be rolled out. Sprinkle top with a very little
bit of flour.

5. Roll from center toward outer edge, lifting rolling pin
just before edge is reached to prevent splitting and cracking of pastry. Repeat several times, following the pattern
of spokes in a wheel, forming pastry into circle 11 to 12
inches in diameter and ⅛ inch thick.

6. Fold pastry circle in half, placing in ungreased pie plate
with fold along center line. Unfold by flipping pastry from
center to side. Repair small breaks or holes by gently press-
ing edges together or using extra pastry for patches. Trim
edges, if uneven, leaving as much edge as possible.

7. *For Unbaked Pie Shell:* Do not prick bottom of crust.
Make filling of choice and fill pie shell. Roll out top crust,
using same method used for bottom crust. Fold pastry in
half along center line over filling, or gently roll pastry
around rolling pin and unroll over filled pie. Even edges
of top crust by trimming with scissors or sharp knife. Fold
edge of bottom crust over top crust. Pinch or press two
together with fingers or fork tines. Prick top crust with
toothpick, or cut small slit or designs with sharp knife to
allow steam to escape. Brush with lightly beaten egg
white, if desired. Bake as directed for individual pie.

8. *For Baked Pie Shell:* Preheat oven to 450°F. Roll out
pastry and place it on pie plate as directed for unbaked
pie shell. Trim ragged edges of pastry to about ½ inch
beyond outer rim of pie plate. Turn edge under and press
against the under side of the rim. Flute, or design the top
edge as desired. Prick bottom of crust with fork tines
deeply and closely. Prick sides once every inch all the way
around. Chill about ½ hour. Bake 12 to 15 minutes. Cool
before filling.

French Apple Pie

6 to 8 servings
Like other fruit and berry pies, this takes a little longer to bake above sea level.

Unbaked 9-inch pie shell
  6 to 8 tart apples, peeled, cored and thinly sliced
  1 teaspoon ground cinnamon
  ¼ teaspoon ground nutmeg

1 cup plus 2 tablespoons all-purpose flour
⅔ cup sugar
½ cup plus 2 tablespoons softened butter
½ cup firmly packed brown sugar

1. Preheat oven to 450°F. Refrigerate unbaked pie shell while preparing apples.
2. In large mixing bowl, combine apples, cinnamon, nutmeg, 2 tablespoons flour and granulated sugar. Mix with apples. Spoon into pie shell. Dot with 2 tablespoons butter.
3. In small bowl, cream remaining ½ cup butter with brown sugar. With pastry blender or spoon, work remaining 1 cup flour into butter-sugar mixture. Sprinkle crumb mixture over apples.
4. Bake at 450°F. for 15 minutes, then *reduce* temperature to 350°F. and bake 35 to 40 minutes more, or until apples are tender.

Black Bottom Pie

6 to 8 servings

9-inch Gingersnap Crumb
   Crust, page 203 (*or*
   gingersnap *or* half
   gingersnaps and half
   chocolate wafers)
1 tablespoon unflavored
   gelatin
2¼ cups cold milk
¾ cup plus 1 tablespoon
   sugar
1½ tablespoons cornstarch

½ teaspoon salt
4 eggs, separated
1 tablespoon rum
1½ ounces melted unsweet-
   ened chocolate
1 teaspoon vanilla extract
¼ teaspoon *fresh* cream of
   tartar
1 cup whipping cream,
   whipped
Shaved chocolate

1. Have ready chilled crumb crust.
2. Soften gelatin in ¼ cup cold milk.
3. In top of double boiler, combine ½ cup sugar, cornstarch and salt. Gradually add remaining 2 cups milk. Cook over boiling water, stirring constantly, until mixture simmers. Cover. Cook, stirring occasionally, for 15 to 20 minutes.
4. Beat egg yolks. Slowly beat some of cooked mixture into egg yolks. Return to hot mixture. Cook, stirring constantly, about 5 minutes. Remove from heat. Divide into two parts.
5. To one half add soaked gelatin, stirring until gelatin is dissolved. Add rum. Cool.
6. Add melted chocolate to remaining half, stirring to blend. Add vanilla extract. Cool. Pour into crumb crust.
7. Beat egg whites with cream of tartar until stiff but not dry. Add remaining sugar a little at a time. With pliable

rubber scraper or whisk, fold stiffly beaten egg whites into gelatin mixture. Pour over chocolate layer in pie shell. Refrigerate until firm.
8. Before serving, spread whipped cream over top and sprinkle with shaved chocolate.

Sour Cream Raisin Pie

6 servings

Pastry for 2-crust, 9-inch pie, page 203
1 cup seedless raisins
Water
1 cup dairy sour cream
¾ cup sugar
1 egg, slightly beaten

1 teaspoon ground cinnamon
½ teaspoon ground cloves
½ teaspoon ground allspice
½ teaspoon salt
3 tablespoons vinegar
Butter
Coffee Cream

1. Preheat oven to 425°F. Line 9-inch pie plate with half of rolled-out pastry.
2. In small saucepan, bring raisins to boil in a little water. Drain.
3. In mixing bowl, combine raisins with all remaining ingredients except butter and coffee cream.
4. Pour into pie shell. Dot with butter. Cover with top crust. Seal edges. Prick crust, or cut slits or designs to allow steam to escape. Brush top crust with cream. Sprinkle with sugar.
5. Bake for 30 to 40 minutes, or until done.

Rhubarb Cream Pie

6 to 8 servings

Pastry for 2-crust, 9-inch pie
  3 cups diced rhubarb
1½ cups sugar
  2 eggs, well beaten
  3 tablespoons all-purpose
    flour

½ teaspoon ground
  cinnamon *or* nutmeg
⅛ teaspoon salt
1 tablespoon butter

1. Preheat oven to 450°F. Line 9-inch pie plate with half of rolled-out pastry.
2. Place rhubarb in pie shell.
3. In small mixing bowl, combine remaining ingredients. Beat until smooth. Pour over rhubarb. Cover with top crust. Seal edges. Prick crust, or cut slits or designs to allow steam to escape.
4. Bake at 450°F. for 10 minutes, then *reduce* temperature to 400°F. and bake 35 minutes more.

Bananas Flambé

4 servings

¼ cup butter
  6 bananas, peeled and cut
    in half lengthwise
¼ cup firmly packed brown
  sugar

¼ teaspoon ground
  cinnamon
½ cup rum

1. In medium-size skillet over low heat, melt butter. Do not brown.

2. Add bananas. Sprinkle 2 tablespoons brown sugar and cinnamon over bananas. Cook, turning once or twice, until soft.
3. Add rum and remaining 2 tablespoons brown sugar. Ignite the rum and stir. Serve at once, with sauce poured over each helping.

Hot Fruit Dessert

8 to 10 servings

1 can (No. 2) peach halves
1 can (No. 2) red plums, pitted
1 can (No. 2) apricot halves
1 can (No. 2) Bing cherries, pitted

¼ cup kirsch *or* brandy
2 tablespoons butter
1½ cups dairy sour cream
½ cup firmly packed brown sugar

1. Drain fruits, reserving juices. Place fruit in 1½-quart baking dish in layers: first peaches, then plums, apricots and cherries. Add kirsch or brandy.
2. Mix fruit juices together and pour just enough into dish to cover fruits. Dot with butter.
3. Preheat oven to 325°F. Bake fruit 20 minutes.
4. Top with sour cream and sprinkle with brown sugar. Serve at once.

Broiled Apricots

18 canned unpeeled apricot halves, drained (reserve juice)

18 canned whole pitted black cherries

¾ cup syrup from apricots

⅓ cup firmly packed brown sugar

3 tablespoons butter

1. Preheat oven to 350°F.
2. Arrange drained apricots, cut side up, in flat baking dish. Place a cherry in center of each apricot.
3. In small saucepan, combine apricot juice, brown sugar and butter. Bring rapidly to boil, stirring to dissolve sugar. Pour hot syrup over apricots.
4. Bake for 10 minutes. Place under broiler for 3 to 4 minutes, or until nicely glazed, basting with juice.

Pears à la Cacao

4 servings
Serve in stemmed sherbet glasses or on lettuce leaves.

1 can (No. 2½) pears, drained (reserve syrup)

⅓ cup syrup from pears

¼ cup crème de cacao

1 cup whipping cream, whipped

Instant coffee powder

1. Chill pears.
2. Combine ⅓ cup pear syrup with crème de cacao.
3. Pour over pears. Chill 3 to 4 hours.
4. Place pears in sherbet glasses or on lettuce leaf. Top with whipped cream. Drizzle with creme de cacao syrup mixture. Sprinkle a little instant coffee powder over each serving.

Enchanted Compote

6 to 8 servings

1 pint fresh raspberries
½ pound seedless white
  grapes
9 fresh peaches, peeled and
  sliced
½ cup sugar

1 teaspoon vanilla extract
1 cup whipping cream,
  whipped
½ cup semisweet chocolate
  bits

1. Wash and prepare fruit. Place in shallow 2-quart baking dish. Gently mix with sugar. Refrigerate.
2. Just before serving, whip cream and add vanilla extract. Spread over fruit. Sprinkle with chocolate bits.
3. Place under broiler, 3 to 4 inches away from flame or element. Broil about 1 minute, or until chocolate starts to melt. Serve at once.

Cakes & Cookies

Elegant Chocolate Cake

12 to 16 servings

the 1st Cake (non-mix)
this is excellent
in ages to succeed
12/41

3 ounces unsweetened
  chocolate
½ cup plus 2 tablespoons
  shortening
1 cup sugar
1 cup firmly packed brown
  sugar
4 eggs, separated (beat
  whites until stiff, but
  not dry)

1 teaspoon baking soda
1½ cups milk *or* 1 cup
  buttermilk
3 cups sifted cake flour
½ teaspoon salt
1 teaspoon vanilla extract
Creamy Chocolate Frosting,
  page 254

1. Preheat oven to 350°F. Grease and flour three 9-inch layer pans, or line with waxed paper and grease.
2. Melt chocolate over simmering water. Cool.
3. Cream shortening with sugars until light and fluffy. Add egg yolks. Beat well. Blend in melted chocolate.
4. Dissolve soda in milk or buttermilk.
5. Mix and sift flour and salt together.
6. Add dry ingredients alternately with milk to chocolate mixture, mixing thoroughly after each addition. Add vanilla extract.

7. With pliable rubber scraper or whisk, gently fold in stiffly beaten egg whites.
8. Pour batter into prepared pans.
9. Bake 30 to 35 minutes, or until center springs back when pressed with fingertip. Cool.
10. Fill and frost with Creamy Chocolate Frosting.

Sacher Torte

8 to 12 servings

The original recipe has never been revealed, but this is a fine adaptation of the Viennese chocolate classic that attracts travelers from around the world to the Hotel Sacher in Vienna.

7 ounces semisweet chocolate
¾ cup softened butter
¾ cup sugar
¼ teaspoon salt
½ teaspoon vanilla extract
8 egg yolks

1 cup sifted all-purpose flour
10 egg whites, beaten until stiff but not dry
¼ cup apricot jam
Chocolate Glaze, page 258
1 cup whipping cream, whipped

1. Preheat oven to 325°F. Generously grease and flour an 8-inch spring-form pan.
2. Melt chocolate over simmering water. Cool.
3. In mixing bowl, cream butter with sugar until light and fluffy. Blend in salt, chocolate and vanilla extract.
4. Add egg yolks one at a time. Beat well after each addition. Gradually add sifted flour to chocolate mixture.
5. With pliable rubber scraper or whisk, gently fold in stiffly beaten egg whites into batter.

6. Spread batter evenly in prepared pan.
7. Bake for 50 to 55 minutes. Cool cake for 15 minutes. Remove pan sides and bottom. Invert cake on wire rack. Let stand until completely cooled.
8. In saucepan, heat apricot jam, stirring frequently until boiling. Remove from heat. Press through fine sieve.
9. Place cake, bottom-side up, on serving plate. Brush top and sides of cake with strained apricot jam. Let stand about 1 hour to allow glaze to set.
10. Frost top and sides with Chocolate Glaze. Refrigerate until frosting has hardened. As is the custom in Vienna, top each serving with a generous dollop of whipped cream.

Sour-Cream Chocolate Cake

About 10 servings
Above sea level, sour cream produces cakes of excellent texture.

3 ounces unsweetened
  chocolate
1 cup sugar
1 cup dairy sour cream
1 egg
1 teaspoon baking soda

¾ cup milk
  2 cups sifted cake flour
½ teaspoon salt
Creamy Chocolate Frosting,
  page 254, if desired

1. Preheat oven to 350°F. Grease and flour two 8-inch layer pans.
2. Melt chocolate over simmering water. Cool.
3. Cream sugar with sour cream. Beat in egg. Add melted chocolate.
4. Dissolve soda in milk.

5. Mix and sift flour and salt together.
6. Add dry ingredients alternately with milk to chocolate mixture, mixing thoroughly after each addition. Batter will seem thin.
7. Pour batter into prepared pans.
8. Bake for about 20 to 25 minutes, or until cake center springs back when pressed with fingertip. Cool.
9. Frost with Creamy Chocolate Frosting, if desired.

Coconut Cake

About 12 servings

1 cup shredded coconut
2 tablespoons milk
¾ cup butter or margarine
1¾ cups minus 1 tablespoon sugar
2¾ cups sifted all-purpose flour
2½ teaspoons double-acting baking powder

½ teaspoon salt
1 cup plus 2 tablespoons water
1 teaspoon lemon extract
4 egg whites, beaten until stiff but not dry
Boiled White Frosting, page 251

1. Preheat oven to 375°F. Grease and flour two 9-inch layer pans.
2. Soak coconut in milk for 5 to 10 minutes.
3. Cream butter or margarine with sugar until light and fluffy.
4. Mix and sift flour, baking powder and salt together.
5. Add dry ingredients alternately with water to creamed mixture, mixing thoroughly after each addition. Add lemon extract and coconut-milk mixture. Blend very well.

6. With pliable rubber scraper or whisk, gently fold in stiffly beaten egg whites.
7. Pour batter into prepared pans.
8. Bake for 25 to 30 minutes, or until cake center springs back when pressed with fingertip. Cool.
9. Fill and frost with Boiled White Frosting. Sprinkle top with additional coconut, if desired.

Dessert Ring

About 12 servings

¾ cup softened butter
1½ cups sugar
2 eggs
1 cup dairy sour cream
1 teaspoon vanilla extract
2 cups sifted cake flour

1 teaspoon double-acting baking powder
¼ teaspoon salt
Cocoa Pecan Topping, page 253
Cream Cheese Frosting, page 252

1. Preheat oven to 350°F. Grease and flour 9 x 4-inch tube pan.
2. Cream butter with sugar until light and fluffy.
3. Add eggs one at a time. Beat well after each addition. Blend in sour cream and vanilla extract.
4. Mix and sift flour, baking powder and salt together.
5. Add dry ingredients a little at a time to creamed mixture, mixing thoroughly after each addition.
6. Spoon batter into prepared pan. Sprinkle Cocoa Pecan Topping over top.
7. Bake for 50 to 60 minutes, or until cake center springs back when pressed with fingertip.

8. Invert pan on wire rack or inverted funnel until cool. Frost with any flavor Cream Cheese Frosting.

Poppy Seed Cake

About 10 servings

¼ to ½ cup poppy seeds
1 cup milk
⅔ cup butter
1½ cups sugar
  2 cups plus 2 tablespoons sifted cake flour
  2 teaspoons double-acting baking powder

½ teaspoon salt
½ teaspoon vanilla extract
4 egg whites, beaten until stiff but not dry
Butter Frosting Supreme, page 249

1. Soak poppy seeds in milk for at least 5 hours in refrigerator.
2. Preheat oven to 375°F. Grease and flour two 8-inch layer pans.
3. Cream butter with sugar until light and fluffy.
4. Mix and sift flour, baking powder and salt together.
5. Add dry ingredients alternately with milk and poppy seeds to creamed mixture, mixing thoroughly after each addition. Add vanilla extract. Mix very well.
6. With a pliable rubber scraper or whisk, gently fold in stiffly beaten egg whites.
7. Pour batter into prepared pans.
8. Bake for about 25 to 30 minutes, or until cake center springs back when pressed with fingertips. Cool.
9. Fill and frost with Butter Frosting Supreme.

Peach or Pineapple Upside-Down Cake

6 to 8 servings
This cake has moisture-retentive qualities that make it keep well.

¼ cup butter
¼ cup firmly packed brown
  sugar

6 to 9 canned peach halves
  or pineapple slices
  (reserve syrup)
6 to 9 maraschino cherries

1. Preheat oven to 360°F.
2. In small saucepan, melt butter and brown sugar together over low heat.
3. Arrange pineapple slices or peach halves (cut side down) on bottom of ungreased 8 x 8 x 2-inch pan, putting cherry in center of each.
4. Cover with brown-sugar mixture.

BATTER

3 eggs, separated (beat
  whites until stiff, but
  not dry)
1 cup sugar
1½ cups sifted all-purpose
  flour

1 teaspoon double-acting
  baking powder
½ teaspoon salt
½ cup syrup from canned
  peaches or pineapple

1. Beat egg yolks well. Gradually add sugar. Beat until blended.
2. Sift flour again. Mix and sift flour with baking powder and salt.
3. Add dry ingredients alternately with syrup to batter, mixing thoroughly after each addition.

4. With pliable rubber scraper or whisk, gently fold in stiffly beaten egg whites.
5. Pour batter over fruit.
6. Bake for 45 minutes, or until center springs back when pressed lightly.
7. Let stand at least 15 minutes. Turn onto plate, fruit side up, to cool.
8. Serve with sweetened whipped cream, if desired.

Powdered-Sugar Cake

About 12 servings

2 cups powdered sugar
⅔ cup softened butter
2½ cups sifted cake flour
2½ teaspoons double-acting
   baking powder
½ teaspoon salt
1 cup plus 1 tablespoon
   milk

1 teaspoon vanilla or
   almond extract
6 egg whites, beaten until
   stiff but not dry
Boiled White Frosting,
   page 251

1. Preheat oven to 350°F. Grease and flour three 8-inch layer pans, or line them with waxed paper and grease paper.
2. Sift powdered sugar over butter. Cream until light and fluffy.
3. Mix and sift flour, baking powder and salt together.
4. Add dry ingredients alternately with milk to creamed mixture, mixing thoroughly after each addition. Add vanilla or almond extract. Blend very well.

5. With pliable rubber scraper or whisk, gently fold in stiffly beaten egg whites.
6. Pour batter into prepared pans.
7. Bake for 25 to 30 minutes, or until cake center springs back when pressed with fingertip. Cool.
8. Fill and frost with Boiled White Frosting.

Edelweiss White Cake

About 12 servings

½ cup butter
1 cup sugar
2 cups sifted cake flour
2½ teaspoons double-acting
   baking powder
¼ teaspoon salt

1 cup milk
1 teaspoon vanilla extract
3 egg whites, beaten until
   stiff but not dry
Cream Cheese Frosting,
   page 252

1. Preheat oven to 350°F. Grease and flour two 8- or 9-inch layer pans.
2. Cream butter with sugar until light and fluffy.
3. Mix and sift flour, baking powder and salt together.
4. Add dry ingredients alternately with milk to creamed mixture, mixing thoroughly after each addition. Add vanilla extract. Mix very well.
5. With a pliable rubber scraper or whisk, gently fold in stiffly beaten egg whites.
6. Pour batter into prepared pans.
7. Bake for 25 to 30 minutes, or until cake center springs back when pressed with fingertip. Cool.
8. Fill and frost with any flavor Cream Cheese Frosting.

Buttermilk Pound Cake

About 16 servings

1 cup softened butter
2 cups sugar
4 eggs
¼ teaspoon almond extract and ¼ teaspoon vanilla extract *or*
2 teaspoons grated lemon rind and 1 tablespoon lemon juice

3 cups sifted all-purpose flour
½ teaspoon double-acting baking powder
¼ teaspoon baking soda
¼ teaspoon salt
1 cup buttermilk

1. Preheat oven to 350°F. Line with waxed paper and butter a 10 x 4-inch tube pan or 10 x 5 x 3-inch loaf pan.
2. Cream butter with sugar until light and fluffy. Add eggs one at a time, beating very well after each addition. Add almond and vanilla extracts, or grated lemon rind and juice.
3. Mix and sift flour, baking powder, soda and salt together.
4. Add dry ingredients alternately with buttermilk to creamed mixture, mixing thoroughly after each addition.
5. Pour batter into prepared pan.
6. Bake 1½ hours, or until cake tester inserted in center comes out clean.
7. Invert pan on wire rack or inverted funnel until cold.

Chocolate Pound Cake: Melt 3 ounces chocolate over hot water; cool. Add to creamed mixture. Substitute 1 teaspoon vanilla extract for almond and vanilla extracts or grated lemon rind and juice.

Banana Cake

About 12 servings
This cake keeps especially well.

1 cup sugar
2¼ cups sifted cake flour
  1 teaspoon double-acting
    baking powder
  ½ teaspoon baking soda
  ½ teaspoon salt
  ½ cup shortening
  ½ cup soured coffee cream
    or ½ cup milk and
    1 teaspoon vinegar or
    lemon juice

1 cup mashed ripe
  bananas
2 eggs
1 teaspoon vanilla extract
⅔ cup chopped nutmeats,
  if desired
Seafoam Frosting, page 252

1. Preheat oven to 375°F. Grease and flour two 9-inch layer pans or a shallow 13 x 9 x 2-inch pan.
2. Mix and sift sugar, flour, baking powder, soda and salt into mixing bowl.
3. Add shortening, soured cream or milk with vinegar or lemon juice, and bananas. Beat 2 minutes with electric mixer set at low or medium speed, scraping bowl sides and bottom frequently; or beat with a spoon until very well blended and smooth.
4. Add eggs and vanilla extract. Beat 2 minutes with mixer, or beat with a spoon until very well blended and smooth. Add nutmeats, if desired.
5. Pour batter into prepared pans.
6. Bake for about 25 to 30 minutes, or until cake center springs back when pressed with fingertip. Cool.
7. Frost with Seafoam Frosting.

Chocolate-Orange Marble Cake

8 to 12 servings

1 ounce unsweetened
chocolate
½ cup butter *or* margarine
1 cup minus 2 tablespoons
sugar
2 eggs
1¼ cups sifted all-purpose
flour
½ teaspoon salt

2 teaspoons double-acting
baking powder
¾ cup milk
1 teaspoon vanilla extract
¼ cup chopped nutmeats
2 teaspoons grated orange
rind
Orange Cream Cheese
Frosting, page 253

1. Preheat oven to 350°F. Grease, line with waxed paper, and grease again a 9 x 3½-inch tube pan.
2. Melt chocolate over simmering water. Cool.
3. Cream butter or margarine with sugar until light and fluffy. Add eggs one at a time, beating well after each addition.
4. Mix and sift flour, salt and baking powder together.
5. Add dry ingredients alternately with milk to creamed mixture, mixing thoroughly after each addition. Add vanilla. Mix very well.
6. Divide batter in half. Gently fold melted chocolate and nutmeats into half of batter. Stir orange rind into other half.
7. Spoon batters alternately into prepared pan.
8. Bake for 50 to 60 minutes, or until cake center springs back when pressed with fingertip. Let stand in pan for 5 minutes before removing to cool.
9. Frost with Orange Cream Cheese Frosting.

Daffodil Yellow Cake

12 to 16 servings

1 cup softened butter *or* margarine

1½ cups sugar

4 eggs, separated (beat whites until stiff, but not dry)

3 cups sifted cake flour

2½ teaspoons double-acting baking powder

½ teaspoon salt

1 cup plus 2 tablespoons milk

2 teaspoons vanilla extract *or* 1 teaspoon grated lemon rind

Butter Frosting Supreme, page 249

1. Preheat oven to 375°F. Grease and flour three 8-inch layer pans, or line them with waxed paper and grease the paper.
2. Cream butter or margarine with sugar until light and fluffy. Add egg yolks. Beat well.
3. Mix and sift flour, baking powder and salt together.
4. Add dry ingredients alternately with milk to creamed mixture, mixing thoroughly after each addition. Add vanilla extract or grated lemon rind. Mix very well.
5. With pliable rubber scraper or whisk, gently fold in stiffly beaten egg whites.
6. Pour batter into prepared pans.
7. Bake for 25 to 30 minutes, or until cake center springs back when pressed with fingertip. Cool.
8. Fill and frost with Butter Frosting Supreme.

Red Velvet Cake

About 12 servings

A unique combination of flavors and ingredients distinguishes this from all other cakes.

½ cup shortening
1½ cups sugar
  3 eggs, separated (beat
    whites until stiff, but
    not dry)
  2 ounces red food coloring
  2 tablespoons cocoa
  2 cups plus 3 tablespoons
    sifted all-purpose flour *or*
2½ cups sifted cake
    flour

1¼ cups buttermilk
  3 teaspoons cherry extract
  1 teaspoon almond extract
  1 teaspoon salt
1½ teaspoons baking soda
    dissolved in 1 tablespoon
    vinegar
Butter Frosting Supreme,
    page 249

1. Preheat oven to 350°F. Line with waxed paper and grease two 9-inch layer pans or a 12 x 8 x 2-inch shallow pan.
2. In mixing bowl, cream shortening with sugar until light and fluffy. Add egg yolks one at a time, beating very well after each addition. Add food coloring and cocoa. Beat well.
3. Add sifted flour alternately with buttermilk to creamed mixture, beginning and ending with flour. Add cherry and almond extracts, salt, and baking soda dissolved in vinegar. Beat well.
4. Pour batter into prepared pans.
5. Bake 20 to 25 minutes for layers; 30 to 35 minutes for sheet cake, or until cake center springs back when lightly pressed. Cool.
6. Frost with Butter Frosting Supreme.

Pumpkin Cake

About 12 servings

½ cup butter
1¼ cups sugar
2 eggs
1 cup canned pumpkin
2¼ cups sifted all-purpose
  flour
1 teaspoon salt
3 teaspoons double-acting
  baking powder
½ teaspoon baking soda

3½ teaspoons pumpkin-pie
  spice, *or* ½ teaspoon
  ground cinnamon,
  ¼ teaspoon ground
  cloves and ¼ teaspoon
  ground nutmeg
¾ cup milk
Butter Frosting Supreme,
  page 249, if desired

1. Preheat oven to 360°F. Grease and flour 12 x 8 x 2-inch pan.
2. Cream butter with sugar until light and fluffy. Add eggs one at a time, beating well after each addition. Blend in pumpkin.
3. Mix and sift flour, salt, baking powder, soda and pumpkin-pie spice together.
4. Add dry ingredients alternately with milk to creamed mixture, mixing thoroughly after each addition.
5. Pour batter into prepared pans.
6. Bake for about 50 minutes, or until cake center springs back when pressed with fingertip. Cool.
7. Frost with Butter Frosting Supreme, if desired.

Spice Cake

About 12 servings
Buttermilk, brown sugar and fruit help keep this cake moist.

¾ cup shortening
1½ cups firmly packed
  brown sugar
3 eggs
2½ cups sifted cake flour
¾ teaspoon baking soda
1 teaspoon salt
1 teaspoon ground
  cinnamon
½ teaspoon ground nutmeg

½ teaspoon ground allspice
1¼ cups sour milk or
  buttermilk
1 cup finely chopped
  nutmeats
1 cup raisins, cooked,
  drained and cut up
Coffee Whipped Cream
  Frosting, page 250

1. Preheat oven to 350°F. Line with waxed paper and grease a shallow 13 x 9 x 2-inch pan or two 9-inch layer pans.
2. Cream shortening with brown sugar until light and fluffy. Add eggs one at a time, beating well after each addition.
3. Mix and sift flour, soda, salt, cinnamon, nutmeg and allspice together.
4. Add dry ingredients alternately with sour milk or buttermilk to creamed mixture, mixing thoroughly after each addition. Stir in nutmeats and raisins.
5. Pour batter into prepared pans.
6. Bake sheet cake for 45 to 50 minutes; layers about 25 minutes, or until cake center springs back when pressed with fingertip. Cool.
7. Frost with Coffee Whipped Cream Frosting.

Whipped Cream Cake

About 10 servings

1 cup whipping cream
3 eggs, separated (beat whites until stiff, but not dry)
1½ cups sifted cake flour
1 cup sugar
⅛ teaspoon salt
1 teaspoon double-acting baking powder
Seven-Minute White Frosting, page 257, if desired

1. Preheat oven to 325°F. Grease and flour two 8-inch layer pans.
2. Chill bowl and beaters. Whip cream until almost stiff. Just before cream gets stiff, beat in egg yolks one at a time.
3. Mix and sift flour, sugar, salt and baking powder together twice. Add to whipped cream mixture, folding in gently but thoroughly.
4. With pliable rubber scraper or whisk, gently fold in stiffly beaten egg whites.
5. Pour batter into prepared pans.
6. Bake for 25 to 30 minutes, or until cake center springs back when pressed with fingertip. Cool.
7. Frost with Seven-Minute White Frosting, if desired.

Angel Food Cake Deluxe

12 to 16 servings

In angel food cakes, it is the air beaten into the egg whites that makes them rise. At high elevations, care must be taken not to beat too much air into the whites, as this will make the cake fall. Gradually folding in sifted flour and sugar is a safeguard against overmixing and produces a fine-textured, moist cake.

1¼ cups egg whites (about 10)
½ teaspoon salt
1½ teaspoons *fresh* cream of tartar
1 teaspoon vanilla extract *or* ½ teaspoon vanilla extract and ½ teaspoon almond extract

1½ cups less 1 tablespoon sugar, sifted twice
1¼ cups sifted cake flour
Whipped Cream Frosting, page 250, if desired

1. Preheat oven to 325°F. Have ready ungreased, *spotlessly clean,* 10 x 4-inch tube pan.
2. Beat egg whites until foamy. Add salt, cream of tartar and vanilla extract or vanilla and almond extracts. Continue beating until egg whites form stiff but moist peaks.
3. Using rubber scraper or whisk, gradually fold in ¾ cup sifted sugar 1 tablespoon at a time.
4. Mix and sift flour with remaining ½ cup sugar three times.
5. Sift ¼ cup flour and sugar mixture over batter. Rotating bowl, gently fold it in with pliable rubber scraper or whisk, using 12 to 15 strokes for each addition. Repeat until all the flour and sugar are folded into the egg whites.
6. Pour batter into prepared pan. Cut through batter several times with scraper or knife, to break up air bubbles.
7. Bake for 45 to 50 minutes, or until cake is delicately brown and center top springs back when lightly pressed. Invert

pan on wire rack or inverted funnel until cold. Remove
from pan.
8. Frost with Whipped Cream Frosting, if desired.

Black Angel Food Cake: In Step 4, reduce flour to 1 cup.
Add ¼ cup cocoa, sifting with remaining flour and sugar.

Spice Angel Food Cake: In Step 4, add ¾ teaspoon ground
mace.

Sponge Cake

About 16 servings
*When making sponge cakes, eggs or egg yolks should not be
overbeaten. The lighter atmosphere, especially above 5,000
feet, allows more expansion from air beaten into eggs or egg
whites.*

8 extra large or 9 medium eggs, separated	**1 tablespoon almond extract**
1½ cups less 2 tablespoons sugar, sifted 5 times	**1½ cups cake flour, sifted 5 times**
½ teaspoon salt	**Cream Custard Filling, page 256**

1. Preheat oven to 275°F. Have ready an ungreased, *spotlessly clean* 10 x 4-inch tube pan.
2. Beat egg whites just until soft peaks form. Gradually beat
   in ¾ cup sugar. Add salt and almond extract.
3. In large separate mixing bowl, beat egg yolks until lemon
   colored. Gradually add remaining sugar. Continue to beat
   until very light in color.

4. With a pliable rubber scraper or whisk, gently fold egg yolks into egg whites. Gently fold sifted flour into egg mixture a little at a time.
5. Pour batter into prepared pan. Cut through batter several times with a knife or scraper to break up air bubbles.
6. Bake at 275°F. for 45 minutes, then *increase* temperature to 325°F. and bake 15 minutes more, or until lightly browned and center springs back when lightly pressed with fingertips.
7. Invert on wire rack or inverted funnel until cold. Remove from pan.
8. Split and fill with any flavor Cream Custard Filling. Sprinkle with powdered sugar.

Gingerbread with Filling

8 to 12 servings

½ cup shortening
½ cup sugar
½ cup light molasses
2 eggs
2 teaspoons baking soda
1 cup boiling water

2½ cups sifted all-purpose flour
½ teaspoon salt
1 teaspoon ground ginger
½ teaspoon ground cloves

1. Preheat oven to 350°F. Grease and flour an 8- or 9-inch-square pan.
2. Cream shortening with sugar until light and fluffy. Blend in molasses. Add eggs one at a time, beating well after each addition.
3. Dissolve soda in boiling water.

4. Mix and sift flour, salt, ginger and cloves together.
5. Add dry ingredients alternately with water to creamed mixture, mixing thoroughly after each addition.
6. Pour batter into prepared pan.
7. Bake for 35 to 40 minutes, or until cake center springs back when pressed. Cool.
8. Split in half and fill.

FILLING

2 packages (3 ounces each) cream cheese

¼ cup half-and-half cream

1 cup pitted, finely chopped dates

¼ cup chopped nutmeats

Combine all ingredients. Spread between layers of cooled gingerbread.

Chocolate, Cherry and Date Cake

About 16 servings

3 eggs, well beaten
½ teaspoon vanilla extract
1 cup sugar
1½ cups sifted all-purpose flour
1½ teaspoons double-acting baking powder
½ teaspoon salt

1 package (6 ounces) semisweet chocolate bits
2 cups chopped nutmeats
1 cup chopped dates
1 cup halved maraschino cherries
Blanched almonds
Chocolate Glaze, page 258, if desired.

1. Preheat oven to 325°F. Grease very well 9 x 3½-inch tube pan, or a 10 x 5 x 3-inch loaf pan.

2. To well-beaten eggs add vanilla extract. Gradually add sugar.
3. Mix and sift flour, baking powder and salt together.
4. Add dry ingredients to egg mixture a little at a time, mixing thoroughly after each addition.
5. Stir in chocolate bits, nutmeats, dates and ¾ cup cherries.
6. Pour batter into prepared pan. Decorate top with almonds and remaining ¼ cup cherries.
7. Bake for about 1½ hours, or until cake center springs back when pressed with fingertip. Invert on rack, remove pan, and cool.
8. Glaze with Chocolate Glaze, if desired.

Mocha Cake

About 10 servings

½ cup shortening
1 cup sugar
2 eggs, separated (beat whites until stiff, but not dry)
2¼ cups sifted all-purpose flour

2 teaspoons double-acting baking powder
½ teaspoon salt
1 cup cold coffee
1 teaspoon vanilla extract
½ cup chopped walnut meats, if desired
Penuche Frosting, page 254

1. Preheat oven to 375°F. Grease and flour two 9-inch layer pans, or line with waxed paper and grease.
2. Cream shortening with sugar until light and fluffy. Add egg yolks. Beat well.

3. Mix and sift flour, baking powder and salt together.
4. Add dry ingredients alternately with coffee to creamed mixture, mixing thoroughly after each addition. Add vanilla extract. Mix very well. Add walnut meats, if desired.
5. With pliable rubber scraper or whisk, gently fold in stiffly beaten egg whites.
6. Pour batter into prepared pans.
7. Bake for 25 to 30 minutes, or until cake center springs back when pressed with fingertip. Cool.
8. Fill and frost with Penuche Frosting.

Chinese Almond Cookies

About 3 dozen

1 cup butter *or* shortening
¾ cup sugar
2 eggs, separated
1 teaspoon almond extract
½ teaspoon salt

2¾ cups sifted all-purpose flour
36 to 40 whole unblanched almonds
1 tablespoon water

1. Preheat oven to 350°F. Have ready ungreased cookie sheet.
2. In mixing bowl, cream butter or shortening with sugar until light and fluffy. Beat in egg yolks, almond extract and salt.
3. Add flour to creamed mixture a little at a time, mixing thoroughly after each addition.
4. Chill dough, wrapped in waxed paper or plastic, for 1 hour.

5. Roll dough into 1½-inch balls. Place on cookie sheet. Flatten each ball slightly and press an almond into its center.
6. Beat egg whites and water together. Brush egg whites over cookies.
7. Bake about 15 minutes, or until golden.

Cottage-Cheese Sandwich Cookies

About 4 dozen

2 cups creamed cottage cheese
¾ cup butter *or* margarine
½ teaspoon salt
2 cups sifted all-purpose flour

1 cup thick preserves (strawberry, cherry, peach *or* grape)
Powdered sugar

1. Preheat oven to 350°F. Have ready ungreased cookie sheet.
2. Press cottage cheese through sieve into mixing bowl. Cream butter or margarine well with cottage cheese and salt.
3. Add flour to creamed mixture a little at a time, mixing thoroughly after each addition.
4. On lightly floured surface, roll out dough ¼ inch thick. Cut into 2-inch rounds. Place half of rounds on cookie sheet ½ inch apart. Put about ½ teaspoon preserves in center of each cookie. Cover with remaining rounds and seal edges together with fingers or fork.
5. Bake for 15 to 20 minutes, or just until lightly browned.

6. Cool on rack, sprinkling with powdered sugar while still warm.
7. For a festive effect, before assembling cookies cut a hole in center of each top round, or use a doughnut cutter.

Date-filled Cookies

About 3½ dozen

1 cup butter *or* ½ cup
   butter and ½ cup
   shortening
1 cup sugar
2 eggs
3 cups sifted all-purpose
   flour

½ teaspoon salt
1 teaspoon baking soda
2 teaspoons fresh cream of
   tartar
Date-Nut Filling, page 257

1. Preheat oven to 350°F. Grease a cookie sheet.
2. In mixing bowl, cream butter, or butter and shortening, with sugar until light and fluffy. Add eggs one at a time, beating well after each addition.
3. Mix and sift flour, salt, soda and cream of tartar together.
4. Add dry ingredients to creamed mixture a little at a time, mixing thoroughly after each addition.
5. On lightly floured surface, roll out dough ⅛ to ¼ inch thick. Cut in 2-inch rounds. Place half of rounds on cookie sheet ½ inch apart. Put 1 teaspoonful of filling in center of each cookie. Cover with remaining cookies. Seal edges with fingers or fork.
6. Bake about 20 minutes, or until done.

Cinnamon Sugar Balls: In Step 2, increase sugar to 1½ cups. Add ½ teaspoon vanilla extract. In Step 5, chill dough, then roll into 1-inch balls. Mix 2 tablespoons each granulated sugar and ground cinnamon. Roll balls in cinnamon-sugar mixture. Place 2 inches apart on cookie sheet. Bake in oven preheated to 400°F. for about 10 minutes.

Kifflings

6 to 8 dozen

1½ cups butter
  6 tablespoons sugar
  2 teaspoons vanilla extract
  ½ teaspoon salt

3¾ cups sifted all-purpose flour
  7 tablespoons ground almonds
Powdered sugar

1. Preheat oven to 350°F. Have ready ungreased cookie sheet.
2. In mixing bowl, cream butter with sugar until light and fluffy. Add vanilla extract and salt.
3. Add sifted flour to creamed mixture a little at a time, mixing thoroughly after each addition. Stir in ground almonds.
4. Shape dough into small balls, half moons or bracelet shapes. Place on cookie sheet.
5. Bake for about 20 minutes, or until very lightly browned around the edges. While still hot roll in powdered sugar.

Macaroons

2½ to 3 dozen

**1 can (8 ounces) almond paste
3 egg whites
1⅓ cups sifted powdered sugar**

1. Preheat oven to 325°F. Line cookie sheet with aluminum foil and grease generously.
2. In mixing bowl, combine almond paste with egg whites. Mix together. Let stand about 15 minutes.
3. Stir until smooth. Add powdered sugar.
4. Drop onto prepared cookie sheet in amounts no larger than a quarter or a half-dollar.
5. Bake 15 to 20 minutes. Cool until slightly warm on cake rack. If cookies stick, loosen with very sharp knife.

Pecan Kisses

About 9 dozen

**6 egg whites
2¼ cups firmly packed
  brown sugar
3 tablespoons sifted
  all-purpose flour**

**½ teaspoon salt
4 cups chopped pecan
  meats**

1. Preheat oven to 350°F. Grease cookie sheet generously.
2. In mixing bowl, beat egg whites until foamy. Add brown sugar gradually. Continue to beat until mixture stands in high, firm but moist peaks.

3. Mix flour and salt together. Slowly fold into egg-white mixture. Fold in pecan meats.
4. Drop by small teaspoonfuls onto prepared cookie sheet.
5. Bake for 10 to 12 minutes.

Shortbread Cookies

About 2 dozen

1 cup softened butter	½ cup cornstarch
1 cup sifted all-purpose flour	½ teaspoon salt
½ cup powdered sugar	½ teaspoon vanilla extract

1. Preheat oven to 300°F. Have ready ungreased cookie sheet.
2. Place all ingredients in mixing bowl. Mix together, but do not whip or overblend.
3. Form dough into 1-inch balls. Place 3 inches apart on cookie sheet. Press with fork to make crisscross design.
4. Bake for about 20 minutes, or until edges of cookies are lightly browned.

Walnut Bars

About 1½ dozen

1 cup sifted all-purpose flour	2 eggs, beaten
¼ teaspoon salt	1 teaspoon vanilla extract
¼ teaspoon baking soda	2 cups chopped walnut meats
2 cups firmly packed brown sugar	

1. Preheat oven to 350°F. Grease and flour 9 x 9 x 2-inch pan.
2. Mix and sift flour, salt and soda together.
3. In mixing bowl, gradually add sugar to well-beaten eggs. Add vanilla extract.
4. Add dry ingredients to sugar mixture a little at a time, mixing thoroughly after each addition. Stir in walnuts.
5. Spread batter in prepared pan.
6. Bake for about 30 minutes.
7. Cool in pan, then cut into squares.

Meringue Squares

About 2 dozen
Butter is a good investment when baking these cookies, as it imparts great flavor.

½ cup butter	1½ cups sifted all-purpose
1 cup sugar	flour
2 eggs, beaten	½ teaspoon salt
½ teaspoon vanilla extract	1 teaspoon double-acting baking powder

1. Preheat oven to 325°F. Grease and flour 8 x 8 x 2-inch pan.
2. In mixing bowl, cream butter with sugar until light and fluffy. Beat in eggs. Add vanilla extract.
3. Mix and sift flour, salt, and baking powder together.
4. Add dry ingredients to creamed mixture a little at a time, mixing thoroughly after each addition. Spread batter into prepared pan. Top with meringue.

MERINGUE

1 egg white, beaten until
stiff but not dry
½ teaspoon vanilla extract

1 cup firmly packed
brown sugar
½ cup finely chopped
nutmeats

1. With pliable rubber scraper or whisk, add vanilla extract to egg white. Fold in brown sugar. Spread over cookie batter. Sprinkle with nutmeats.
2. Bake for 30 minutes.
3. Cool. Cut into squares.

Pfeffernuesse

5 to 6 dozen

4½ cups sifted all-purpose
flour
2 teaspoons double-acting
baking powder
½ teaspoon salt
1 tablespoon ground
cinnamon
1 teaspoon ground cloves
½ teaspoon ground nutmeg
¼ teaspoon black pepper

½ teaspoon ground
cardamom seed
½ teaspoon ground anise
seed
1 cup finely chopped citron
1 teaspoon grated lemon
rind
4 eggs
2 cups sugar
Powdered sugar
Milk

1. Preheat oven to 350°F. Have ready ungreased cookie sheet.
2. Sift together into large mixing bowl the flour, baking

powder, salt, cinnamon, cloves, nutmeg, pepper, cardamom and anise seed. Stir in citron and lemon rind.

3. In separate bowl, beat eggs with sugar until thick and
lemon colored. Gradually add to flour and fruit mixture.
Chill dough, well wrapped, at least 2 hours, or overnight.

4. Roll dough into 1¼-inch balls. Place on cookie sheet.

5. Bake 15 to 20 minutes. Glaze while warm with powdered
sugar mixed with a little milk.

6. Cool. Stored in airtight container, these improve with
keeping.

Candies, Frostings, Fillings & Toppings

Hawaiian Fudge

1¼ pounds

The quickened concentration of liquid and sugar where the air is thinner and drier hastens scorching of candy syrups.

2 cups sugar
½ cup coffee cream *or*
  evaporated milk
½ cup drained, crushed
  pineapple
2 tablespoons light corn
  syrup

1 tablespoon butter
Few drops green food
  coloring, if desired
¼ cup chopped nutmeats

1. Butter a 9 x 5 x 3-inch loaf pan.
2. In heavy 3-quart saucepan, combine sugar, cream or evaporated milk, pineapple, corn syrup and butter. Stir over low heat until sugar dissolves. Cook, stirring occasionally, until a small quantity dropped into cold water forms a soft ball, or until correct reading for your altitude is reached on candy thermometer (see table, page 18). Add food coloring, if desired. Cool until lukewarm.

3. Beat until candy is creamy and has lost its gloss. Add nutmeats. Pour into prepared pan (do not scrape pan sides, as scrapings may make candy sugary). When firm, cut into squares.

Butter Crunch

1½ to 2 pounds
Variations in altitude and sudden barometric changes have a noticeable effect on candy-making.

1 cup butter
1⅓ cups sugar
2 tablespoons light corn syrup
3 tablespoons water
¼ teaspoon salt

1 cup coarsely chopped blanched almonds, toasted
16 ounces semisweet chocolate pieces
1 cup finely chopped blanched almonds, toasted

1. Butter a 13 x 9 x 2-inch pan. Have ready 2 sheets of aluminum foil or waxed paper.
2. Melt butter in heavy 2-quart saucepan. Add sugar, corn syrup, water and salt. Cook over low heat, stirring occasionally, until a small quantity dropped into cold water reaches the hard-crack stage, or until correct reading for your elevation is reached on a candy thermometer (see table, page 18). (Watch carefully after temperature reaches 270°F. to prevent scorching.) Remove from heat. Quickly stir in coarsely chopped nutmeats.
3. Spread in prepared pan. Cool completely.

4. In top of double boiler over simmering water, melt chocolate, stirring fast and steadily so it melts evenly. Set aside.
5. Turn cooled candy onto aluminum foil or waxed paper. Coat top with half of melted chocolate. Sprinkle with half of finely chopped almonds.
6. Cover closely with aluminum foil or waxed paper. Invert quickly. Peel off foil or waxed paper. Spread with remaining chocolate and sprinkle with remaining almonds.
7. Refrigerate until firm. Break into pieces and store in airtight container.

Unforgettable Candied Fruit Peel

About 1 pound

4 grapefruit, bright-colored, thick-peeled and unblemished *or* 6 large navel oranges *or* 8 large lemons	2 cups sugar 1 cup water Few drops red and green food coloring, if desired Sugar

1. Wash grapefruit, oranges or lemons. Remove peel in 2 sections. Cut each section into ¼-inch strips.
2. In saucepan large enough to accommodate easily all the peel, add cold water to cover. Bring to boil. Cook 10 minutes. Drain. Repeat three times, cooking 4 times in all; drain. Cover again with boiling water. Simmer until tender. Drain.
3. In heavy 2-quart saucepan with cover, combine sugar and water. Cook over low heat, stirring constantly, until sugar is dissolved. Boil for a few minutes. Add peel. Cover and cook slowly until syrup thickens.

4. For clear-colored peel continue to cook until syrup is practically absorbed. For colored peel, divide peel and syrup before final cooking into two equal parts in two saucepans. Add a few drops green food coloring to one pan and a few drops of red coloring to the other. Cook until peel is evenly colored and syrup is practically absorbed.
5. Generously sprinkle a large tray with granulated sugar. Remove peel strips from pan with fork and roll each in sugar until thoroughly coated. (Or put generous amount of granulated sugar in paper bag, put drained peel strips in bag, and shake until peel is thoroughly coated.)
6. Separate coated strips and dry on wire rack; or place in oven at 250°F. until surface is firm. Store in air-tight container.

Caramels

About 1½ pounds

2 cups sugar	1½ cups chopped pecan
1¾ cups light corn syrup	meats
½ cup butter	½ teaspoon salt
2 cups coffee cream	1 teaspoon vanilla extract

1. Butter 8-inch square baking pan.
2. In heavy 4-quart saucepan combine sugar, corn syrup, butter and 1 cup cream. Cook over low heat until mixture boils. Add remaining 1 cup cream gradually without interrupting boiling. Cook, stirring constantly with wooden spoon, until a small quantity dropped into cold water forms a firm ball, or until correct reading for your eleva-

tion is reached on candy thermometer (see table, page 18). Remove from heat. Stir in pecan meats, salt and vanilla extract.
3. Pour into prepared pan to depth of ¾ to 1 inch. Cool.
4. When firm, cut into squares. Wrap individually in plastic wrapping or waxed paper.

Chocolate Caramels: In Step 2 substitute 1 cup firmly packed brown sugar for granulated sugar. Add 3 ounces unsweetened chocolate.

Panocha

(*Panoche or Penuche*)   About 1½ pounds

2 cups firmly packed brown sugar and 1 cup granulated sugar *or* 3 cups firmly packed brown sugar	¼ teaspoon salt
	1 tablespoon butter
	1½ teaspoons vanilla extract
	¾ cup chopped pecan or walnut meats
1 cup coffee cream *or* evaporated milk	

1. Lightly butter a 9 x 5 x 3-inch loaf pan.
2. In heavy 3-quart saucepan cook sugar, cream or evaporated milk and salt over low heat, stirring constantly, until sugar is dissolved. Cook, stirring constantly, until a small quantity dropped into cold water forms a soft ball, or until correct reading for your altitude is reached on candy thermometer (see table, page 18). Remove from heat.
3. Add butter; do not stir. Set aside and cool to lukewarm. Add vanilla extract.

4. With wooden spoon, beat until thick and creamy. Add nutmeats. Turn into prepared pan.
5. When completely cooled, cover pan and let stand over-night at room temperature. Cut into squares. Store in air-tight container.

Mexican Penuche: In Step 4, add ½ cup finely chopped figs.

Peanut Penuche: In Step 4, substitute peanuts for pecan or walnut meats.

Butter Frosting Supreme

Filling and frosting for three 8- or 9-inch layers
Make half of this recipe for a sheet cake or a two-layer cake.

5 tablespoons cake flour	½ teaspoon salt
1 cup milk	1¾ cups sifted powdered
1 cup softened butter	sugar
1 cup sugar	½ cup coarsely chopped
1 teaspoon vanilla extract	nutmeats, if desired

1. In top of double boiler, gradually blend together flour and milk. Cook over boiling water, stirring constantly, until mixture forms a thick, nearly stiff, paste. Cool.
2. In mixing bowl, cream butter with sugar until very light and fluffy. Add cooled paste, vanilla extract, and salt. Beat until smooth.
3. Fill cake with one third of mixture.
4. Add powdered sugar to remaining two thirds. Add nut-meats if desired. Blend well. Spread on top and sides of cake.

Whipped Cream Frosting, Filling or Topping

Filling and frosting for two 8-inch layers
The basic recipe also makes an exciting filling, sometimes called Chantilly Cream, for meringue shells (page 194). (The cornstarch in powdered sugar acts as a stabilizer when using flavorings in whipped cream mixtures, as does the gelatin.)

½ teaspoon unflavored
  gelatin
1 tablespoon cold water
1 cup whipping cream

¼ cup powdered sugar
⅛ teaspoon salt
½ teaspoon vanilla extract

1. In cup, soak gelatin in cold water.
2. Scald 2 tablespoons whipping cream. Pour over gelatin, stirring until dissolved. Cool.
3. Whip remaining cream. Add sugar, salt and vanilla extract. Stir in gelatin mixture.

Coffee Whipped Cream Frosting, Filling or Topping: In Step 3, add 1 to 2 teaspoons instant coffee powder.

Mandarin Orange Whipped Cream Frosting, Filling or Topping: In Step 3, add 1 can (11 ounces) well-drained mandarin orange sections and 1 tablespoon cognac or ½ teaspoon grated orange rind.

Strawberry Whipped Cream Frosting, Filling or Topping: In Step 3, gently add 2 cups sliced, drained strawberries, 2 tablespoons fresh chopped mint, or 2 tablespoons Cointreau or orange juice. Increase powdered sugar to ½ cup. Prepare and use shortly before serving time.

Syracuse Whipped Cream Cake Frosting, Filling or Topping:
In Step 3, add 9 finely chopped candied cherries, 6 finely
chopped large marshmallows and 4 dried and crumbled
macaroons.

Boiled White Frosting

Filling and frosting for three 9-inch layers

3 egg whites	1 tablespoon light corn
2¼ cups sugar	syrup
¼ teaspoon salt	½ cup water
	1 teaspoon vanilla extract

1. In top of double boiler, combine egg whites, sugar, salt,
   corn syrup and water.
2. Cook over boiling water, beating continually with electric
   mixer set at high speed, until frosting holds shape when
   beater is raised and is of a consistency for spreading. Do
   not let frosting crystallize. Add vanilla extract.

Boiled Lemon Frosting: Substitute ¼ cup lemon juice for
¼ cup water. Substitute 1 teaspoon grated lemon rind for
vanilla extract.

Boiled Orange Frosting: Substitute ½ cup orange juice for
water. In Step 2, add ¼ teaspoon *fresh* cream of tartar
and 8 marshmallows, quartered. Substitute ½ teaspoon
grated orange rind for vanilla extract. Fold marshmallows
into cooked mixture immediately after removing from
heat, stirring until partially dissolved.

Boiled Peppermint Candy Frosting: In Step 2, add 1 cup crushed peppermint candy.

Lady Baltimore Frosting: In Step 2, add ⅓ cup chopped, dried figs, ⅔ cup pitted, chopped dates, and ½ cup chopped white raisins after removing from heat.

Lord Baltimore Frosting: In Step 2, add ½ cup toasted coconut, ½ cup chopped candied cherries, and ¼ cup chopped pecan meats after removing from heat.

Seafoam Frosting: Substitute brown sugar for granulated sugar, and dark corn syrup for light, if desired.

Cream Cheese Frosting

Filling and frosting for two 8- or 9-inch layers
Cheese acts as a moisturizer as well as imparting subtle flavor. Ingredients easily halved for smaller cakes.

2 packages (3 ounces each) cream cheese	4 cups sifted powdered sugar
4 tablespoons coffee cream	¼ teaspoon salt
2 tablespoons softened butter	1 teaspoon vanilla extract

1. In mixing bowl, beat cream cheese, cream, and butter together until fluffy.
2. Gradually add powdered sugar. Add salt and vanilla extract.

Chocolate Cream Cheese Frosting: In Step 1, add 2 ounces melted, unsweetened chocolate.

Coffee Cream Cheese Frosting: In Step 2, add 3 to 4 teaspoons instant coffee.

Cranberry or Tart Jelly Cream Cheese Frosting: Substitute cranberry or any tart jelly for cream.

Lemon Cream Cheese Frosting: Substitute lemon juice for cream and grated lemon rind for vanilla extract.

Orange Cream Cheese Frosting: Substitute orange juice for cream, and grated rind for vanilla extract.

Strawberry Cream Cheese Frosting: Substitute ⅓ cup mashed strawberries for cream.

Cocoa Pecan Topping

Topping for one 9-inch cake or coffee cake

2 tablespoons firmly packed brown sugar
1 teaspoon instant cocoa mix *or* ½ teaspoon cocoa and ½ teaspoon sugar

½ teaspoon ground cinnamon
½ cup chopped pecan meats

1. In small mixing bowl, mix all ingredients thoroughly.
2. Sprinkle over top of cake or coffee-cake batter when ready to bake.

Creamy Chocolate Frosting

Frosting for a 14- by 9-inch sheet cake or two 9-inch layers

[handwritten: not good to enough to apply again try 12/71]

2 ounces unsweetened
chocolate
4 tablespoons water
6 tablespoons butter

2 egg yolks, beaten
½ teaspoon salt
1 box (1 pound) powdered
sugar, sifted

1. In top of double boiler, melt chocolate, water and butter together over simmering water. Cool. Add beaten egg yolks and salt.
2. Place top of double boiler directly on medium-low heat and bring to boil. Cook 2 minutes, stirring constantly.
3. Remove from heat. Blend in powdered sugar. Beat well until of a consistency for easy spreading.

Penuche Frosting

Filling and frosting for two 8- or 9-inch layers

¾ cup sugar
¾ cup firmly packed brown
sugar
½ cup butter
½ cup vegetable shortening
½ cup milk

¼ teaspoon salt
1 tablespoon light corn
syrup
1 teaspoon vanilla extract
1 cup chopped nutmeats

1. In heavy saucepan combine sugars, butter, shortening, milk, salt and corn syrup. Cook over low heat to full rolling boil, stirring constantly. Boil 2 minutes.
2. Cool until lukewarm. Add vanilla extract. Beat until of consistency for spreading. Add nutmeats.

Streusel Topping

Enough for 12 to 15 muffins or sweet yeast rolls, or one 10-inch coffee cake

2 tablespoons all-purpose flour	½ cup firmly packed brown sugar *or* ½ cup sugar
2 teaspoons ground cinnamon	2 tablespoons melted butter
	½ cup chopped pecan or walnut meats

1. In mixing bowl, blend flour, cinnamon and sugar together. Work in butter. (The mixture will be crumbly and dry.) Add chopped pecan or walnut meats.
2. Sprinkle over top of unbaked batter or dough.

Marmalade Topping: In Step 1, increase flour to 4 tablespoons and add ¼ cup orange marmalade and 1 tablespoon cream. Omit cinnamon. During baking, this topping will sink into batter.

Cinnamon Nut Filling

Filling for about 1 dozen sweet rolls or 9-inch coffee cake

⅓ cup sugar	1 cup chopped nutmeats
1 egg, beaten	Milk
1 teaspoon ground cinnamon	

1. In 1-quart saucepan combine all ingredients, adding enough milk to thicken paste to proper consistency for spreading. Boil about 1 minute to blend well.
2. Cool before using.

Cream Custard Filling

Filling for three 8-inch cake layers or 6 cream puffs or éclairs

¾ cup sugar
5 tablespoons all-purpose
   flour *or* 3 tablespoons
   cornstarch
¼ teaspoon salt

2 cups scalded milk
2 eggs, beaten
1½ teaspoons vanilla extract
1 cup whipping cream,
   whipped (if desired)

1. In heavy 1-quart saucepan, mix together sugar, flour or cornstarch, and salt. Over low heat, gradually stir in scalded milk.
2. Bring to boil slowly, stirring constantly. Remove from heat.
3. Stir a little hot mixture into beaten eggs, then gradually stir egg mixture into hot mixture.
4. Cook over low heat, stirring constantly and vigorously for 3 minutes. (Custard should hold shape on end of lifted spoon when done.)
5. Cool. Add vanilla extract. Fold in whipped cream, if desired, just before using.

Coffee Cream Custard Filling: In Step 1, add 2 teaspoons instant coffee powder to scalded milk; or substitute 1 cup cream and ½ cup strong brewed coffee for milk. For more pronounced flavor, increase strength of coffee or add more powder to taste.

Sherry or Rum Cream Custard Filling: In Step 5, substitute 1 tablespoon sherry or rum for vanilla extract.

Date-Nut Filling for Sweet Yeast Rolls, Coffee Cakes and Cookies

Filling for 2 dozen rolls, 2 coffee cakes or 5 dozen cookies

½ cup sugar
½ cup water

1¼ cups pitted, chopped dates
2 cups chopped nutmeats

1. In heavy 1-quart saucepan, cook sugar, water and dates over low heat until slightly thickened.
2. Add nutmeats. Cook about 5 minutes more. Remove from heat. Cool.

Seven-Minute White Frosting

Filling and frosting for two 8-inch cake layers

1 extra large or 2 small egg whites
⅞ cup sugar
3 tablespoons cold water

¼ teaspoon *fresh* cream of tartar
2 tablespoons light corn syrup
½ teaspoon vanilla extract

1. In top of double boiler, combine egg white, sugar, water and cream of tartar.
2. Cook over boiling water, beating continually with electric mixer or rotary beater, for 7 minutes, or until frosting holds shape when beater is raised and is of consistency for spreading.
3. Remove from heat. Add vanilla extract. Spread while hot on thoroughly cooled cake.

Chocolate Seven-Minute Frosting: In Step 1 add 1 ounce unsweetened chocolate, melted and cooled.

Lime Seven-Minute Frosting: In Step 1, substitute 1 tablespoon lime juice for 1 tablespoon water. In Step 3, use 1 tablespoon grated lime rind instead of vanilla extract.

Chocolate Glaze

Glaze for top of an 8- or 9-inch cake or 1 dozen doughnuts or éclairs

2 tablespoons butter	2 tablespoons powdered
2 ounces unsweetened	sugar
chocolate	⅛ teaspoon salt

1. In top of double boiler, blend together all ingredients.
2. Cook over simmering water, stirring until smooth.
3. Use while warm.

Freezing, Canning, Pickling & Preserving

Blue Ribbon Dill Pickles

About four quart jars

Do not pack cucumbers too tightly in jars, as each quart must have at least 1½ cups of vinegar mixture to keep pickles safely.

30 to 40 cucumbers (3-inch size)
12 sprigs fresh dill, with seeds
12 small hot red peppers
4 cloves garlic

½ teaspoon powdered alum
4 grape leaves, if desired
2 quarts cider vinegar
1 quart water
1 cup coarse salt

1. Have hot sterilized jars ready. (See Sterilizing, page 14.)
2. Scrub cucumbers. Do not cut off ends.
3. Place sprig of dill in bottom of each jar. Pack cucumbers into jars, distributing among them 3 red peppers and 1 clove garlic to each jar. Place another sprig of dill in center of cucumbers and another on top. Add ⅛ teaspoon alum to each jar and place a grape leaf on top, if desired.
4. In large enamel or stainless-steel saucepan, combine vinegar, water and salt. Bring to boil. Fill jars with boiling vinegar mixture. Seal. Pickles are better if allowed to ripen several weeks before serving.

Apple-Mint Chutney
About eight 8-ounce jars

2 cups vinegar	½ cup finely chopped fresh
2 pounds apples	mint leaves
¾ pound seedless raisins	1 ounce white mustard seed
2 red peppers	¼ cup salt
6 small onions	2 cups sugar

1. Boil vinegar in small saucepan for 2 minutes. Cool.
2. Grind apples, raisins, peppers and onions together into large bowl. Add boiled vinegar, chopped mint, mustard seed, salt and sugar. Stir until sugar is dissolved.
3. Place in crock with cover. Store in cool place.
4. Stir each morning for 10 days.
5. Pack in sterilized jars. (See Sterilizing, page 14.) Seal.

Watermelon Pickles
Four 8-ounce jars

1 large watermelon	1 teaspoon ground *or* 1
1 cup salt	tablespoon whole allspice
4 quarts water	1 teaspoon ground *or* 1
2 cups cider vinegar	tablespoon whole cloves
6 cups sugar	1 lemon, sliced
1 teaspoon ground *or* 2 sticks	
cinnamon (2-inch)	

1. Trim dark green skin and pink meat from rind. Cut rind into 1-inch cubes or rounds. Place in large bowl with salt and 4 quarts water. Soak overnight.
2. Drain rind. Rinse in cold water. Place in heavy large enamel or stainless steel saucepan. Cover with cold water.

3. Bring to boil. Cook over low heat just until tender. Drain.
4. In same saucepan, combine 2 cups water, vinegar and sugar. Add ground spices or whole spices tied in bag, and lemon. Boil 5 minutes. Add watermelon rind. Cook over medium-low heat until rind is transparent. Remove spice bag.
5. Pack into hot sterilized jars. (See Sterilizing, page 14.) Seal.

Chili Sauce

About twenty 8-ounce jars

20 pounds ripe tomatoes, washed
Boiling water
  2 pounds onions, peeled
  1 dozen medium-green peppers, washed and seeded
  8 cups sugar
  1 cup salt

1 tablespoon ground allspice
1 tablespoon ground cinnamon
1 tablespoon ground cloves
1 tablespoon ground red pepper
8 cups vinegar

1. Immerse tomatoes in boiling water for 1 minute or until skins slip off easily. Remove skins.
2. Finely chop tomatoes, onions, and green peppers. Place in large enamel or stainless-steel saucepan. Add sugar and salt. Boil 30 minutes.
3. Put spices in small bag. Add spices and vinegar to vegetable mixture.
4. Cook, stirring frequently, until thickened, or about 2 to 3 hours depending on the juice in the tomatoes.
5. Pour into sterilized jars. (See Sterilizing, page 14.) Seal.

Port Wine Jelly

About six 6-ounce glasses

3 cups sugar
2 cups port wine
½ bottle (3 ounces) liquid
fruit pectin

¼ teaspoon crumbled dried
rosemary, if desired

1. In large enamel or stainless-steel saucepan, combine sugar and wine.
2. Heat, stirring constantly, until sugar is dissolved. Increase heat and bring to full, rolling boil. Boil 1 minute, stirring constantly. Add liquid pectin, and rosemary, if desired. Bring again to full, rolling boil. Boil 1 minute. Remove from heat. Skim off froth.
3. Pour through fine sieve into hot, sterilized glasses. (See Sterilizing, page 14.) Seal with thin layer of paraffin.

Cranberry Port Wine Jelly: In Step 1, reduce port wine to 1 cup. Add 1 cup cranberry juice. In Step 2, substitute cinnamon for rosemary.

Grape Port Wine Jelly: In Step 1, reduce port wine to 1 cup. Add 1 cup grape juice. In Step 2, omit rosemary. Add ¼ teaspoon each cinnamon and nutmeg.

Black Raspberry Jelly

6 cups black raspberries,
washed
Juice of 1 lemon

1 cup sugar for each 1 cup
black raspberry juice

1. Crush a layer of black raspberries in bottom of large enamel or stainless-steel saucepan. Add remaining berries.

2. Cook over low heat, stirring occasionally, until moisture begins to be drawn from the berries. Increase heat to medium-low. Cook until berries are soft, or about 5 to 10 minutes.

3. Remove from heat. Pour cooked fruit into dampened jelly bag or layers of cheesecloth in sieve or colander.

4. Measure no more than 4 cups juice into large heavy saucepan. Add lemon juice. Bring juice to boiling. Skim off froth. Add 1 cup sugar for each 1 cup black raspberry juice. Stir over medium-low heat until sugar is dissolved. Heat to boiling. Cook without stirring until point of jelling. (See Jellies, page 12.)

5. Pour into hot sterilized glasses. (See Sterilizing, page 14.) Seal with thin layer of paraffin.

Black Raspberry or Red Raspberry and Apple Jelly: In Step 4, use 1 part black or red raspberry juice and 2 parts apple juice.

Citrus Marmalade

About eight 8-ounce glasses

2 oranges	8 cups water
1 lemon	12 cups sugar
1 grapefruit	

1. Wash fruit. Slice, and remove seeds. Grind together.

2. Place ground fruit in large bowl. Add water and let stand in cool place for 24 hours.

3. Pour fruit and its juice into large enamel or stainless-steel saucepan. Simmer over low heat 1 hour. Add sugar and stir until dissolved. Bring to low boil. Cook 30 minutes.

4. Pour into hot, sterilized jars or glasses. See (Sterilizing, page 14.) Seal with lids or thin layer of paraffin.

Pineapple-Apricot Jam
Four 8-ounce glasses

2 cups dried apricots,
rinsed and drained
2½ cups water

2 cups canned crushed
pineapple and juice
½ lemon, sliced
4 cups sugar

1. Place apricots and water in large enamel or stainless-steel saucepan. Cover and simmer over low heat until tender.
2. Mash apricots. Add pineapple and juice, lemon slices and sugar.
3. Cook over medium-low heat, stirring frequently to prevent scorching, until thickened and clear. (See Jellies, page 12.)
4. Pour into hot sterilized jars or jelly glasses. (See Sterilizing, page 14.) Seal with lids or a thin layer of paraffin.

Spiced Peaches
About 2 quarts

10 medium peaches
Boiling water
3 tablespoons lemon juice
5½ cups water
6 tablespoons finely
chopped onion

2 teaspoons ground
cinnamon
5 cups sugar
1 cup white vinegar
12 whole cloves

1. Immerse peaches in boiling water for 1 minute, or until skins slip off easily. Remove skins. Place in solution of lemon juice mixed with 4 cups water to prevent darkening.
2. In 3-quart saucepan, combine remaining 1½ cups water, onion, cinnamon, sugar, vinegar and cloves. Bring to boil. Add peaches. Cook over medium heat about 10 minutes.
3. Loosely pack peaches in sterilized hot jars. (See Sterilizing, page 14.) Cover with syrup. Seal.

Peach Conserve

About eight 8-ounce jars or glasses

12 peaches, washed
6 oranges, washed
⅞ cup sugar for each 1 cup fruit

1 cup chopped maraschino cherries, if desired

1. Immerse peaches in boiling water for 1 minute, or until skins slip off easily. Remove skins.
2. Coarsely grind peaches and oranges together. Measure. Place in large enamel or stainless-steel saucepan. Add ⅞ cup sugar for each 1 cup fruit. Stir until sugar is dissolved.
3. Cook over medium-low heat, stirring frequently to prevent scorching, until thickened, clear, and a spoonful dropped on a dish will hold shape. Add cherries, if desired.
4. Pour into hot sterilized jars or jelly glasses. (See Sterilizing, page 14.) Seal with lids or thin layer of paraffin.

Index

Albert sauce, 156
almond cookies, Chinese, 235–6
almondine sauce, 154
anchovy sauce, 156
angel food cake, deluxe, 229–31; black, 231; spice, 231
anise-seed bread, 55
antelope, venison or elk: marinated, 144; pot roast, 143
appetizers, 7, 34–40; beef tenderloin and Canadian bacon, planked, 35–6; Braunschweiger pâté, 34–5; Camembert-Roquefort mousse, 38; cheese puffs, 38–9; chili con queso, 39; cocktail: burgers, 37, kebobs, broiled, 36–7; meat balls, 37; mushrooms, stuffed, 39–40; shrimps gourmet, 40
apple: mint chutney, 260; pie, French, 206
apricot(s): broiled, 211; pineapple jam, 264; sour-cream rolls, 61; stuffing, 165–6
Armenian lamb casserole, 121–2
artichoke(s): Italiana, 177–8; salad: plate, 169; stuffed, 169
asparagus Parmigiana, 178–9

baking powder, 7
banana(s): cake, 223; flambé, 209–10
barbecue sauce, 154–5
batter, high-country fish, 94–5
Bavarian beef rolls, 118
beans, green, with dill, 177
béarnaise sauce, 157
béchamel sauce, 155

beef: Bavarian rolls, 118; boiled, with horseradish, 110–11; Chinese ginger, 115–16; Danish meat balls with mashed potatoes, 113–14; East Indian curry, 116–17; enchiladas, 84–5; kal dolmar, 117; meat loaf with herbs, 114; pot roast, 109–10; roasting, high-altitude timetable for, 19; Sauerbraten, 112–13; sirloin tips Émile, 111–12; stock, 46–7; Stroganoff, 115; tenderloin and Canadian bacon, planked, 35–6
beets in orange sauce, 180
beverages, 41–4; chocolate: hot, spiced, 41–2; Mexican, 42; coffee, 9–10, 41; mulled Burgundy wine, hot, 42; punch: cranberry, hot, 42; fruit, all-season, 43–4; rum fruit, 44; Spanish wine, 43; sangría, 43; tea, 14, 41
bigarade, sauce, 163
black bottom pie, 207–8
Black Forest lamb shanks, 122
black raspberry jelly, 262–3; or red raspberry and apple jelly, 263
blueberry: pancakes, 72–3; supreme, 193–4
boiled beef with horseradish, 110–11
boiled frosting: Lady Baltimore, 252; lemon, 251; Lord Baltimore, 252; orange, 251; peppermint candy, 252; seafoam, 252; white, 251–2
boiling, 7
borscht, 44–5
braising, 7

fish (*continued*)
fillet of, 97; herbed stuffing for,
168; poached, 95; red snapper
Caribbean, 99–100; sole or flounder
Romano, fillet of, 97–8; soufflé, 92;
stock, 94; tuna or salmon noodle
casserole, 100; *see also* shellfish
flounder or sole Romano, fillet of,
97–8
flour, 11
foil cookery, 11
frankfurters, Southwestern, 118–19
freezing, 11
French: apple pie, 206; leeks, 185;
veal stew, 128–9
fresh pork, roasting, high-altitude
timetable for, 20–1
fricasseeing, 11
fritters, 10: fruit or berry, 71–2
frogs' legs Provençale, 99
frostings and fillings, 11, 249–58:
boiled: Lady Baltimore, 252;
lemon, 251; Lord Baltimore, 252;
orange, 251; peppermint candy,
252; seafoam, 252; white, 251–2;
butter supreme, 249; chocolate
glaze, 258; cinnamon nut, 255;
cocoa pecan topping, 253; cream
cheese frosting, 252–3: chocolate,
252; coffee, 253; cranberry or tart
jelly, 253; lemon, 253; orange, 253;
strawberry, 253; creamy chocolate,
254; date-nut, 257; marmalade, 255;
penuche, 254; seven-minute white,
257–8: chocolate, 258; lime, 258;
Streusel, 255; whipped cream,
250–1: coffee, 250; Mandarin
orange, 250; strawberry, 250;
Syracuse, 251
fruit: or berry fritters, 71–2; dessert:
frozen, 201; hot, 210; gelatin,
frosted, 172; punch: all-season,
43–4; rum, 44
fudge, Hawaiian, 244–5
fumet, 94

game, 11, 143–7: antelope, venison or
elk: marinated, 144; pot roast, 143;
elk, venison or antelope:
marinated, 144; pot roast, 143;
rabbit: Italienne, 146–7; smothered
with fruit juice, 145–6; venison,
elk or antelope: marinated, 144;
pot roast, 143; steaks or chops,
pan-fried, 145

game birds, 11, 147–53; dove breasts,
baked, 147; partridge, stewed, 152;
pheasant in sauce, roast spiced,
153; teal, roast, 149; wild duck:
maison, 149–50; roast, I, 148;
II, 148–9; wild goose, roast:
I, 150–1; II, 151; pique-nique,
151–2; wild rice stuffing for, 167
gazpacho, 53
ginger beef, Chinese, 115–16
gingerbread, 232–3
glazes: for baked ham, 165; honey,
165
gnocchi, 80–1: with tomato sauce, 81
Gorgonzola cheese dressing, 174
grape port wine jelly, 262
gravies, 12
green mayonnaise, 164
green pepper(s): sauce, 159–60;
stuffed, 179–80: cheese, 180;
shrimp, 180
ground beef in cabbage leaves, 117
gumbo, shrimp, crab or oyster, 47–8

halibut, baked fillet of, 97
ham: glaze for bakes, 165; loaf, 124;
noodle and green-pepper casserole,
123–4; roasting, high-altitude
timetable for, 20–1
hashed brown potatoes with
nectarines, 191
Hawaiian: barbecued lamb steaks or
chops, 120–1; fudge, 244–5;
vegetable tempura, 176
herbed stuffing for fish, 168
hominy and almond casserole, 79
honey glaze, 165
horseradish sauce, 156
Hungarian veal birds, 129–30

Irish buttermilk bread, 64–5

jalapeño spoon bread, 65–6
jellies and jams, 12, 262–5: black
raspberry, 262–3; or red raspberry
and apple, 263; citrus marmalade,
263–4; peach conserve, 265;
pineapple-apricot, 264; port wine,
262: cranberry, 262; grape, 262;
red, 262

kal dolmar, 117
kebobs: broiled cocktail, 36–7;
lobster and tenderloin, 102

About the Authors

Beverly Anderson Nemiro and Donna Miller Hamilton are the undisputed authorities on cooking at high altitudes. They have co-authored the classic *The Complete Book of High Altitude Baking*, as well as *Colorado à la Carte* and *Where to Eat in Colorado*.

Beverly Anderson Nemiro was born in St. Paul, Minnesota. She attended Reed College in Oregon and took her B. A. degree in journalism at the University of Colorado. She has had a career in teaching, free-lance writing and fashions, succeeding Mrs. Hamilton as fashion director of a Denver department store.

She is married to Jerome M. Nemiro, president of May-D & F department store and has three children. Mrs. Nemiro is active in community work and is a Denver tennis champion and an avid skier. She continues her writing, publishing articles in a number of national magazines. With Marie Von Allmen, she co-authored *Lunch Box Cookbook* and is currently working on another cookbook.

Donna Miller Hamilton comes from a pioneer Colorado family. She was educated in the Denver public schools and attended extension divisions at the University of Colorado and the University of Denver. She has had a career in advertising, fashions, and foods. She left her position as fashion director at a Denver department store to devote more time to her family, her writing and community affairs.

She is married to Darrell J. Hamilton, an insurance executive and has five children. She is a member of the board of trustees of The Children's Hospital in Denver and of the Denver Zoological Foundation. Mrs. Hamilton has her own television program called "High Country Cooking," which gives a fresh approach to the perennial problem of feeding the family.